A Report From the Clinton-Gore Administration

Building Livable Communities

Sustaining Prosperity, Improving Quality of Life, Building a Sense of Community

Revised
June 2000

Photos courtesy of: Lynn Betts, Liesel Duhon, Patricia Evans, Ron Nichols, USDA Natural Resources Conservation Service, and Environmental Protection Agency

For sale by the U.S. Government Printing Office
Superintendent of Documents, Mail Stop: SSOP, Washington, DC 20402-9328

ISBN 0-16-050397-3

Thomas Clarke
2001

TABLE OF CONTENTS

FOREWORD

We all want economic prosperity and a high quality of life for our families, regardless of where we live or what we do for a living. Across America, a new movement is emerging as citizens work together to build more quality into their lives and make their communities more livable. What are livable communities? People want neighborhoods with safe streets and good schools. They want good jobs that aren't hours away from home. They want housing they can afford and neighborhood parks where children can play. They want to get to work or run errands without spending hours in traffic. They want clean air to breathe and clean water to drink. They want to live in a place that feels like a community.

In many places, these simple things are becoming hard to find. One reason is that some communities have been growing in ways that detract from a high quality of life. That form of growth is sometimes called sprawl – or uncoordinated growth. Sprawl encourages disinvestment in older urban and suburban neighborhoods, while causing property taxes in new suburbs to soar to pay for new roads, schools, and public services. It threatens farmland and open space while polluting our air and our water. It creates traffic congestion because driving is often the only way to get where you want to go.

Many communities are realizing that sprawl is not inevitable. These communities have moved beyond divisive pro-growth and anti-growth arguments to embrace *smart growth*. Across the country, communities are pursuing smart growth strategies to build more livable communities. In 1998 and 1999, voters resoundingly approved hundreds of state and local ballot measures to encourage smarter growth. This is not a partisan issue, nor should it be. Elected officials of both parties, with the vision and experience to help communities make appropriate local choices, have led the way.

This broad support demonstrates that these issues touch the lives of almost every American. Business leaders understand that the availability of affordable housing, good transportation systems, and a high quality of life is a competitive advantage in attracting a skilled work force. Urban and suburban residents recognize that reinvesting in cities can revitalize older communities while preserving the quality of life in suburban areas. Farmers realize that smart growth policies can relieve development pressures that can force them from their land. People everywhere view smart growth as a way to reduce traffic congestion and protect open space.

This report describes the challenges of dealing with sprawl and celebrates a "wave of local innovation" as Americans work together to improve the quality of life in their communities. This report also defines an appropriate role for the federal government in these efforts. If you start with the fundamental principle that *communities know best*, the role of the federal government is straightforward: support locally driven efforts to build more livable communities. The Livable Communities Initiative presented here is a comprehensive package that demonstrates that the federal government can be a supportive partner with communities seeking to grow in ways that ensure a high quality of life and strong, sustainable economic prosperity in the 21st century.

Al Gore

Vice President Al Gore

June 2000

INTRODUCTION

Over the last seven and one-half years, the policies of the Clinton-Gore Administration have helped produce the strongest economy in a generation. In 1992, wages were stagnant, the unemployment rate was 7.5 percent, and the federal government was running deficits as far as one could see. Today, the United States is enjoying what is now the longest economic expansion in U.S. history.

Since President Clinton took office, the economy has added more than 21 million new jobs and the unemployment rate is near four percent – the lowest rate in more than 30 years. Americans have had five consecutive years of real wage growth, exploding federal deficits have been turned into surpluses, and crime rates have fallen for eight consecutive years. Across America, communities are thriving: employment is up, crime is down, and local budgets are in the black.

New challenges, however, lie ahead. Even as communities welcome and benefit from this extraordinary economic resurgence, many of them – from our cities to suburbs to small rural towns – worry that their prosperity and quality of life are threatened. They see much more traffic congestion and much less open space. They see prime farmland usurped by development while usable land in the city sits idle. Too often, the growth they are experiencing is the kind known as "sprawl."

The Administration has launched an effort to help all communities meet these challenges – the Livable Communities Initiative. Its aim is to provide communities with tools, information, and resources they can use to enhance their residents' quality of life, ensure their community's economic competitiveness, and build a stronger sense of community.

Our goal is to help build livable communities for the 21st century – to develop places where older neighborhoods thrive once again; where you can walk safely on the streets; where historic neighborhoods as well as farms, forests, and other green spaces are preserved; where Americans spend less time in traffic and more time with their children, spouses, and neighbors; where homes are safe and secure from nature's forces; and all can share in our prosperity. We want to develop places with good schools, clean environments, and public and private spaces that help foster a spirit of community.

Federal policies can influence patterns of growth – often, inadvertently – and their possible contribution to sprawl is a matter of some debate. With the Livable Communities Initiative, the Administration seeks to ensure that the federal government works *with* communities to build futures that:

- Sustain prosperity and expand economic opportunity;
- Enhance the quality of life; and
- Build a stronger sense of community.

The Livable Communities Initiative contains an array of existing and proposed programs and policies to help communities meet these objectives. It offers communities resources and tools they can use to revitalize urban neighborhoods, ease traffic congestion, preserve farmland and open spaces, become disaster resistant, address the distribution of environmental burdens and benefits, and achieve equitable development. Through collaboration among neighboring jurisdictions, smart growth planning, and engagement of the private sector, these programs can help improve air and water quality, clean up abandoned brownfields, and improve traffic safety.

The Livable Communities Initiative recognizes the importance of investing in places and is founded on community-based solutions. It is based on the notion that *communities know best*. Every community is different. Decisions about how they grow are best made by the communities themselves. Therefore, it is the responsibility of the federal government to assist and to inform, not direct. As a result, the Livable Communities Initiative defines four primary roles for the federal government in building livable communities:

- Expanding Community Choices by Providing Incentives;
- Expanding Community Choices by Providing Information;
- Being a Good Neighbor; and
- Building Partnerships.

At the request of Vice President Gore, this report identifies concrete steps the Administration is taking to help communities grow in ways that ensure a high quality of life and strong, sustainable economic prosperity. It includes a brief description of challenges faced by urban, suburban and rural communities, the innovative ways in which some are meeting them, and our Livable Communities Initiative – a comprehensive package of 30 policy actions and voluntary partnerships that support local efforts to build livable communities.

More detailed information on available programs, tools and resources, and how communities can put them to use, can be found on the Internet at <www.livablecommunities.gov>.

GROWTH: NEW CHALLENGES AND OPPORTUNITIES

A NEW AMERICAN LANDSCAPE

Historically, America's cities have been places of promise. People from small towns and rural areas were drawn to the city in search of economic opportunity. In their heyday, America's cities were works of *civic* art. At the heart of our cities, we created impressive public areas – town halls, libraries, post offices, parks, and plazas – and created a sense of pride. In the shops and on the street corners, neighbors shared the news of the day and forged a sense of community. Factories located in cities to take advantage of the ready supply of labor. Upon the common ground of our cities, Americans of all walks of life worked, played, learned, worshipped, and practiced the art of democracy.

But, the American landscape has undergone profound transformations in the past 50 years. After World War II, more and more city dwellers left their compact urban neighborhoods – which many had come to view as crowded, dirty, and noisy – in pursuit of a new American Dream. They found this dream in newly built suburbs on the city's edge, which offered affordable homes with yards, safe streets, good schools, and ready access to green spaces where families could relax.

Spurred by the prosperity of the post-war era – and the resulting availability of affordable transportation – this outward migration began a fundamental shift in American patterns of development. Previously, America's population grew quickly but our "footprint" on the land spread slowly. Since the mid-1900s, however, population growth has slowed, while the amount of land committed to development has rapidly increased. To illustrate, between 1970 and 1990, the population of the Los Angeles metropolitan region grew 45 percent while developed land increased by almost 300 percent. During the same time period, the Chicago metropolitan population grew by only four percent while land use soared by 46 percent. Much of this growth in the amount of land used is due to the tendency toward single-use development, putting greater distance between residential, retail, and employment centers.

For many, our current patterns of growth have indeed delivered a high quality of life with good schools, economic prosperity, affordable housing, low crime, and access to nature. But for many others – from the inner city to older suburbs to small rural towns – the results are mixed. As investment is diverted from the urban core, blighted urban neighborhoods continue to suffer from crime, high unemployment, and a lack of basic services. As valuable farmland is converted to malls and subdivisions, rural communities struggle to sustain their economies and way of life. And as development pushes farther out, residents of older suburbs find themselves confronting many of the "urban" ills they sought to escape, while residents of newer suburbs find themselves mired in traffic and saddled with the escalating taxes needed to pay for services and infrastructure in the new developments.

Although often not apparent, the challenges confronting urban, suburban, and rural communities are in many ways interrelated. But they cannot simply be ascribed to the fact that developed land is growing faster than population. Rather, these problems are more closely associated with *how* we grow – too often, haphazardly, building roads, houses, malls, and office parks without anticipating how they all fit together, without making an appropriate assessment of the impact to the environment, without making sure that they provide the foundation for true neighborhoods and communities.

The expansion of developed land has also placed increased demands on natural resources. Across America, communities struggle each day with issues ranging from air pollution, to loss of wetlands, to having enough clean water for their citizens. In particular, water is inextricably linked to the health of communities. An adequate supply of clean water is absolutely vital for communities to enhance their present livability and plan for future sustainable development. Indeed, the growth of some communities in the West and elsewhere is already significantly constrained by the availability of new water resources.

This constellation of concerns – haphazard development patterns, disinvestment in older communities, and deteriorating quality of life – can be described in many ways. To many it is known simply as "sprawl." Confronting it poses both challenges and opportunities for urban, suburban, and rural communities.

Challenges to Our Cities

As investment and attention moved out of central cities after World War II, a cycle of decline took hold in many urban areas. Disinvestment in urban infrastructure and amenities – such as schools, parks, and transit systems – made some urban neighborhoods less desirable places to live. Many middle class citizens left, eroding the tax base and undermining the cities' fiscal strength and vitality, allowing crime to increase, roads and sewers to age, school quality to decline, and urban blight to worsen. Racial tensions increased. Taxes on remaining residents increased and services declined. Over time, once vibrant commercial areas suffered. Businesses closed. Industrial sites were abandoned. Jobs were lost. While many cities survived and some even thrived during this time, in many places, opportunity gave way to despair.

As businesses and middle-class residents moved out, they left behind a disproportionate number of low income families who lacked the resources to move. Those unable to leave were not provided ample opportunity to obtain well paying jobs or high quality education. These families were left with a depleted tax base that could not sustain city services. The Department of Housing and Urban Development's 2000 State of the Cities Report found poverty rates are falling in cities but are still twice that of suburbs. While the country at large is enjoying the longest peacetime economic expansion in American history, large swaths of our cities seem to have been left out. The share of central city population that is low-income has grown from 21.9 percent in 1969 to 25.5 percent in 1998. More than 10 percent of city residents live in neighborhoods where 40 percent or more of the households are below the poverty line with all the associated social problems of crime, drugs, poor healthcare, failing schools, environmental degradation, and substandard housing. And, although crime has decreased throughout America, crime rates remain higher in cities than in other areas.

Common among these poorer neighborhoods are pockets of disinvestment, neglect, and abandonment known as "brownfields." Brownfields are abandoned or underutilized properties where redevelopment is complicated by real or perceived industrial contamination. The General Accounting Office estimates that there are more than 450,000 such sites in the United States. The U.S. Conference of Mayors, which has called for a national commitment to recycle the thousands of brownfields in America's cities, finds that redevelopment of these areas could generate 550,000 additional jobs and up to $2.4 billion in new tax revenue for cities. One of the keys to revitalizing urban neighborhoods is targeting investment in these neglected properties as a way of drawing new businesses and catalyzing a sustainable economic recovery.

America's cities have long been troubled. Yet the revitalization of urban America now seems possible due to a growing awareness that our cities represent significant untapped retail, land, and labor markets. If this revitalization should occur, a major challenge will be ensuring that current residents of distressed communities share in – and are not displaced by – this new prosperity.

Challenges to Suburban Areas

Abandoned and underutilized buildings and declining economic activity are not limited to cities. Indeed, many older suburban communities are now falling victim to the same cycle of decline.

When first built, these suburbs provided middle-class Americans the opportunity to own homes in safe, clean, and pleasant surroundings. Families moved to them in search of a higher quality of life. But new development kept moving farther out, surrounding many of these areas with strip malls and eliminating their connections to open space. Many of these communities were built quickly with little regard to how they would age over time. In 1961, author Jane Jacobs, a long-time observer of urban America, presciently claimed that such places "lack any reasonable degree of innate vitality," adding that "few of them, and these only the most expensive as a rule, hold their attraction much longer than a generation."

While suburban communities continue to offer affordable housing and other amenities many Americans seek, Jacobs' prediction has proven true in many older suburbs. These suburbs could not compete for residential investment with new suburban areas on the ever-expanding fringe. With middle-class homebuyers often avoiding these older suburbs, property values dropped and residents moved farther out.

Many of the strip malls that characterized commercial development in these older suburbs could not compete for customers with the new enclosed malls in the outer suburbs. Richard Moe and Carter Wilkie, in *Changing Places: Rebuilding Community in the Age of Sprawl*, refer to the "boarded-up first-generation shopping centers" as the "new suburban slums." They note that of the five billion square feet of retail space in the United States, "half a billion sits empty, the equivalent of more than four thousand abandoned shopping centers or 'dead malls.'"

As the cycle of decline spread outward from the urban core, these aging suburbs began to experience many of the same problems as the cities. Household incomes dropped, crime increased, schools became troubled, signs of blight were apparent – all of which accelerated the move to yet more distant suburbs. David Rusk, an urban expert and the former mayor of Albuquerque, described this phenomenon in the Cleveland region:

> **Barely two decades ago, inner suburbs such as Euclid, Lakewood, and Maple Heights boasted above average household incomes. Now they've sunk 10 to 20 percentage points below the regional average as higher-end households move out to new subdivisions in farther out Geauga, Lake, and Portage Counties.**

Newer suburbs, meanwhile, are encountering their own challenges – chief among them, traffic congestion and rising property taxes.

As we spread farther out, Americans must travel greater distances between home, work, shopping, and recreation. Yet in many communities, transportation choices have narrowed rather than expanded. As a result, families depend on cars for more of their daily travel. By 1995, according to the Department of Transportation's National Personal Transportation Survey, more than four of every five household trips were unrelated to work. Total miles driven have also soared. Since 1980, census figures show that the U.S. population has grown one percent a year. Meanwhile, according to the Bureau of Transportation Statistics, vehicle-miles traveled (VMT) has risen 3.2 percent a year. Put another way, the total number of miles driven by Americans each year is increasing more than three times as fast as the country's population.

While cars have afforded us unprecedented mobility, increased driving contributes to chronic air pollution, despite tremendous advances in emission controls. It also adversely affects water quality as the paving required for additional roads and parking lots results in increased polluted runoff to streams, degrading fish and wildlife habitats and often increasing the threat of flooding.

Increased driving puts a strain on family life as well. Indeed, more and more Americans are concluding that they spend too much time in traffic and too little time at home. A 1999 study by the Surface Transportation Policy Project, *High Mileage Moms,* found that on a typical day, the average mother spends more than an hour driving, traveling 29 miles and taking more than five trips.

Our patterns of development are also squeezing the family budget. Many families move to the suburbs in search of affordable housing, only to discover that the anticipated savings are eroded – or overwhelmed – by increased transportation costs and rising property taxes.

Once, a second car was a luxury. But today, many families must own, maintain, and insure two or more cars simply to meet their daily transportation needs. According to the Bureau of Labor Statistics, transportation rose from the third highest expense in the family budget in 1961, at 15.2 percent, to the second highest expense in 1995, at 18.6 percent. According to the Bureau's Consumer Expenditure Survey for 1998, the typical American household earns $41,622 a year and spends $11,841 on housing, $6,785 on transportation, $5,011 on food, and $1,973 on health care. In other words, the typical family spends almost as much on transportation as on food and health care combined.

In a recent change at least partly fueled by a reaction to worsening congestion, Americans are increasingly using public transportation. An April 2000 report by the American Public Transportation Association found that the number of people using mass transit is the largest in 40 years – some nine billion trips last year – and that public ridership is now increasing faster than automobile use.

New development can also hit suburban families in the pocketbook by driving up local property taxes. Paying for sprawl in suburban areas often increases taxes as the required infrastructure and services – roads, sewer, water, schools, and police and fire protection – must be paid for. A study this year by Climate Solutions concludes that every time a family moves into a new home in the Puget Sound region of Washington, the cost of providing these types of services amounts to $20,000 to $30,000, much of which is passed on to all taxpayers. A December 1999 report by *Grow Smart Rhode Island* estimates that over the next 20 years sprawl will cost Rhode Island taxpayers nearly $1.5 billion. More than half of the cost is attributed to tax revenue losses in urban centers. In the last 34 years, Rhode Island has developed more residential, commercial, and industrial land than it did in its first 325 years.

As costs are passed on to existing residents in the form of higher property taxes, many communities are encountering resistance to property tax increases, particularly those areas that have been unable to attract sufficient commercial enterprise to lighten some of the local residential tax burden. Some communities are responding by limiting future residential development, or by establishing "impact fees" requiring developers and new homeowners to bear more of the infrastructure costs of new development.

Challenges to Rural Areas

One of the most profound – yet least appreciated – impacts of current development patterns is the erosion of environmental, cultural, and economic attributes in rural America.

Many families choose rural communities because of their proximity to open space. Farms and forestland provide jobs and opportunities for recreation and a connection to the land. They also provide a variety of environmental benefits, such as flood reduction, groundwater recharge, and wildlife habitat. But in many areas, current growth patterns threaten this "green infrastructure" and many of the intrinsic values and human enterprises sustained in rural communities.

Preliminary results of the Department of Agriculture's 1997 National Resources Inventory show that the national rate of forest, cropland, and open space being converted to urban and other uses has increased dramatically. Areas pressured by development include some of the most productive farmland in the country. Far from being niche areas of production, more than half of U.S. agricultural output by value comes from farms located near urban or suburban centers. According to the American Farmland Trust, about 79 percent of the total United States' production of fruit, 69 percent of the vegetables, 52 percent of the dairy products, 28 percent of the meat, and 27 percent of the grain are produced in counties where rapid development is occurring.

With continuing advances in science and technology pushing agricultural productivity to new heights, these cropland losses have not translated into a net loss in total farm output. Nevertheless, the impacts on individual communities can be devastating. The 1996 farmland protection plan of Suffolk County, New York, estimates that for every dollar paid in property taxes, a farm uses 30 cents in services, while a residential property uses $1.23 in services. So as agricultural land is developed, property taxes rise to support the increased demand for services. Tax rates are often based on a property's value for residential or commercial development, not its current use or the owner's ability to pay. The cycle continues as rising property values and taxes create strong economic pressures for still more farmers to sell their land for development.

Facing the Challenges Together

Our development patterns have an impact on the lives of Americans from coast to coast – from city centers to farms on the fringe of metropolitan areas. City residents wonder about equitable development and if the jobs and opportunities from reinvestment and revitalization will materialize. Suburban residents worry about rising tax rates and find they are spending too much time in traffic, surrounded by too much asphalt and too little green space. Rural residents see their way of life endangered as urban areas encroach, bringing higher taxes and covering the good earth with concrete.

Surveying this vast American landscape, it might not be immediately apparent that these many challenges intersect – that disappearing farmland is linked to poverty in the inner city or to the frustrations of a suburban commuter caught in endless traffic. It's not always easy to see the way that our lives are intertwined. But the boundaries between city, suburb, and countryside are often more imaginary than real. Understanding and acting upon this insight is both a challenge and an opportunity for America's communities.

A WAVE OF LOCAL INNOVATION

Effective responses to the challenges and opportunities posed by sprawl cannot originate from the federal government. They must arise in communities across the nation as concerned citizens join in partnership with civic and business leaders.

Indeed, a wave of local innovation already is sweeping across America. Communities and regions are taking creative steps to tackle economic, social, environmental, and safety challenges posed by our new patterns of development. This wave of community-based activity was described in the

1998 report of the National Commission on Civic Renewal, chaired by William Bennett and former Senator Sam Nunn:

> **Within the neighborhoods, the towns, the local communities of America are the stirrings of a new movement of citizens acting together to solve community problems. It is a nonpartisan movement that crosses traditional jurisdictions and operates on a shoestring. It is a movement that begins with civic dialogue and leads to public action.**

In many cases, communities are making progress not by treating their problems in isolation, but by reaching out to partners in their neighborhoods and regions. New partnerships are emerging in multiple places as cities, suburbs, and rural areas begin to work together, recognizing that their problems – such as abandoned brownfields in cities and the loss of open space in the outer suburbs – are linked. Other partnerships emerge as private sector and community-based groups join together with civic leaders to tackle the economic, social, safety, and environmental challenges facing their communities.

Some communities are beginning to question common assumptions about growth and development. While growth is essential to our continued economic prosperity, the individuals and communities involved in these partnerships are beginning to evaluate the costs of current growth patterns. They are questioning the economic costs of abandoning infrastructure in the city, only to rebuild it in the suburbs. They are questioning costs to our quality of life from ever-increasing traffic congestion. In other words, people and communities are trying to distinguish between types of growth that prevent and solve problems from those that cause problems. They want to promote sustainable growth – growth of jobs, wages, educational achievement, and time with family – but not growth of pollution, poverty, travel time, crime, or taxes.

Those who make such distinctions are not "no growth" advocates or even "slow growth" advocates. They want the jobs, revenues, and amenities that development can provide. But they want it without degrading their environment, unduly raising their local taxes, or diminishing their quality of life. And, they are beginning to believe that continuing our current development patterns won't achieve these goals. They are in the vanguard of a consensus emerging at the community level in support of a better way to grow: *smart growth.*

Smart growth represents efforts to promote new patterns of development that are:

- *Economically smart* because they build upon past investments in existing communities; do not require heavy tax increases in suburban areas to pay for new public services; reduce congestion and thereby increase personal time; and preserve prime farmland for agricultural use.
- *Environmentally smart* because they encourage the redevelopment of brownfields sites; reduce threats to air quality, water quality, and open space; and reduce the impact of natural disasters.
- *Socially smart* because they promote economic opportunity, equitable development, and encourage a "sense of community" within localities and across regions by bringing citizens, businesses, and governments together to solve common problems.

Once the province of a small group of citizen activists, smart growth efforts have blossomed into a broad-based movement intent upon improving America's communities. As the National Association of Home Builders observed:

> **The concept of Smart Growth has exploded onto the national consciousness as one of the most critical issues confronting America today. It touches on choices we Americans hold close to our hearts – where we live, work and play, the education of our children, commute times to work, and the economic and job opportunities created by new growth in our communities. It is an idea that addresses the questions of how best to plan for and manage growth, when and where new residential and commercial development as well as schools and major highways should be built and located and how to pay for the infrastructure required to serve a growing population.**

Local and State Smart Growth Efforts

Proof that smart growth efforts are spreading across the country can be found in the results of recent fall elections. In 1998 and 1999, voters across the country approved more than 300 ballot measures addressing growth-related concerns. In New Jersey, voters overwhelmingly approved $1 billion in expenditures over 10 years to preserve half of the state's remaining open space and amended the state's constitution to provide a stable source of funding. In Pennsylvania, the $650 million "Growing Greener" bill was signed to fund the protection of farmland and open space and additional public and community land use initiatives. Voters in Michigan approved $675 million in bonds for brownfields cleanup, parks, and urban waterfront redevelopment. In Florida, $3 billion will be provided over the next 10 years for acquiring and maintaining land for recreation and preservation. In total, voters approved more than $9 billion in these two elections for conservation, parklands, and smart growth.

This new movement didn't materialize overnight. For several years, new partnerships have been emerging as concerns about sprawl have grown. The breadth of these new partnerships was demonstrated in 1995 when four very different organizations – the Bank of America, the State of California's Resource Agency, the Greenbelt Alliance, and the Low Income Housing Fund – jointly produced *Beyond Sprawl: New Patterns of Growth to Fit the New California.* The groundbreaking report declared that:

> **One of the most fundamental questions we face is whether California can afford to support the pattern of urban and suburban development, often referred to as 'sprawl,' that has characterized its growth since World War II.**
>
> **...This is not a call for limiting growth, but a call for California to be smarter about how it grows – to invent ways we can create compact and efficient growth patterns that are**

responsive to the needs of people at all income levels, and can also help to maintain California's quality of life and economic competitiveness.

In the five years since the release of this landmark report, cities, counties, and towns across the nation are pioneering a wide range of innovative efforts to make their communities more livable:

- **Aquidneck Island, Rhode Island.** Residents realized that open space on the island was disappearing, traffic congestion increasing, and the bucolic character of the island vanishing. In response, the Aquidneck Island Partnership – a collaborative effort of local organizations committed to fostering economic development that enhances the natural and social resources of the island – developed a report illustrating islanders' vision for the future. In addition, the Partnership is working to develop a formal re-use plan for over 400 acres of Navy land and 10 miles of Narragansett Bay shoreline.
- **Moline, Illinois**. On the banks of the Mississippi River, this former industrial manufacturing center is experiencing a rebirth. Facing economic decay, business leaders from Moline established an innovative public-private partnership, Renew Moline, to attract businesses to the downtown riverfront. Deere & Company, the world's largest farm equipment manufacturing company, provided leadership and resources to the partnership which developed John Deere Commons, a major new waterfront complex that is drawing jobs and visitors back to downtown Moline.
- **Tillamook County, Oregon.** Coastal development in Tillamook County has impacted salmon populations and increased the economic costs of seasonal flooding. In the past two years, local officials have integrated planning efforts and used improved decision support tools to direct limited resources to the areas of greatest impact, and coordinate federal, state, and local actions. Because of better information and planning, a recent flooding incident in the county saw a 96 percent reduction in damages. Tillamook County has discovered that what is best for the environment can also be best for citizens and municipal budgets – supporting livability through smart growth, healthy ecosystems, and more disaster resistant communities.
- **Charlotte, North Carolina.** The Bank of America and Cousins Properties Incorporated, the nation's largest office development real estate investment trust, are investing $350 million to develop Gateway Village. Gateway Village is a 15-acre downtown technology and retail center where thousands of Bank of America employees will work and hundreds of people will live. The project will contribute strongly to the revitalization of Charlotte's economy by providing one million square feet of workspace for 3,500 Bank of America employees. Over 230 apartments and condominiums will be available to employees who choose to live close to where they work.
- **Minneapolis, Minnesota**. The Green Institute originated from an environmental justice movement in Minneapolis against the siting of a large garbage transfer station in a residential area of the Phillips neighborhood. In the early 1980s, a 10-

acre site was razed to make room for a garbage transfer station, but Phillips residents fought the plan and ultimately prevailed. Residents then turned their attention to a more sustainable vision for the vacant site and the greater community. The Green Institute now runs innovative businesses that sell used building and construction materials, disassemble buildings, and salvage materials for reuse, creating jobs and keeping construction debris out of landfills. Today, a 64,000-square-foot commercial-industrial facility is located on the site originally intended for the garbage transfer station, housing both the Institute and another 10 to 15 environmentally friendly businesses.

- **Silicon Valley, California.** The Silicon Valley Manufacturing Group, a trade association representing over 130 of the largest Silicon Valley employers, has become actively involved in addressing the unintended impacts of sprawl on Silicon Valley businesses and employees. Between 1995 and 1999, the group successfully advocated for 74 new housing developments in 14 Silicon Valley cities, representing more than 24,000 new homes. The group is participating in an effort to raise funds to establish Silicon Valley's Housing Trust Fund, as well as conducting an inventory of vacant and underused land in the Valley to identify further housing opportunities. The Silicon Valley Manufacturing Group pursues opportunities to increase transportation choices and improve air quality among its member companies by initiating voluntary efforts to reduce mobile source emissions, including ridesharing, bicycle projects, and telecommuting.
- **Cleveland, Ohio.** Until recently, the once flourishing Glenville neighborhood in the heart of Cleveland consisted of broken asphalt, weeds, and condemned buildings. But local civic and business leaders had the vision to build a major retail center to bring investment dollars and pride back to the neighborhood. Today, the new 45,000 square foot Glenville Town Center is taking shape in what was once a jigsaw puzzle of 10 parcels. The Center will open later this year as the home to six national and regional businesses and an array of 14 local restaurants, service, and retail stores.
- **Tucson, Arizona.** Last year, the city of Tucson, working with local developers and the federal Partnership for Advancing Technology in Housing, inaugurated a new 2,600-unit housing development with a pedestrian-friendly design and homes that will use half the energy of typical new homes in the area. The community worked together to craft regulations to encourage design of a mixed residential, commercial, and light industrial development that is an attractive place to live and work and offers enormous environmental benefits.
- **Silver Spring, Maryland.** Public and private dollars are working in combination to help Silver Spring develop a downtown area and become a more competitive business center with a diverse economy operating 24 hours a day, seven days a week. In 1999, a combination public-private investment of approximately $320 million was committed for a three-year period to develop more than one million square feet of residential, retail, restaurants, theaters, hotel, and office space that

will surround public facilities and outdoor gathering places to make the downtown a new center of commerce and community activity for Silver Spring.

- **Gallatin County, Montana.** Gallatin County, a gateway community to Yellowstone National Park, is undergoing rapid population growth. County officials are using geographic information systems to develop a master plan for future development. By managing information better, using new tools to visualize development trends, and gathering citizen input, this rural county has built a community consensus among agricultural, conservation, and business interests for improved land use planning.
- **Miami-Dade County, Florida.** Four non-profit organizations, together with governmental and private sector partners, are leading a community effort to revitalize and transform the 79th Street Corridor in Miami-Dade County from a fragmented set of residential, commercial, and industrial sites with a reputation as dangerous and undesirable into a cohesive neighborhood. By creating transit-oriented development around the confluence of three significant rail and commuter rail lines, this initiative will provide greater access to jobs, services, and amenities for neighborhood residents. Building on other projects in the surrounding neighborhood, the initiative also will expand opportunities for safe, decent, and affordable housing and serve as a catalyst for a new style of neighborhood development in South Florida that builds an environment which addresses the needs of current residents.

States share land use responsibilities with local communities, and a growing number are launching innovative programs to encourage and support local smart growth efforts:

- **California**. Phil Angelides, State Treasurer of California, has led a movement to mobilize the state's financial resources to promote smart growth. Marking a fundamental shift in state policies that govern the flow of billions of dollars, Angelides' Smart Investment plan contains several programs to assist community development and disadvantaged homebuyers. Since the announcement of the effort in June 1999, about $10 billion in investment and capital has been focused on smart growth initiatives. In addition, in May 2000 the Treasurer announced another major policy initiative called the Double Bottom Line. This initiative calls for the direction of more than $8 billion in investment capital to spur economic growth in California's emerging markets – those communities left behind in the state's current economic boom.
- **Massachusetts.** Governor Paul Cellucci issued an executive order directing state agencies, whenever they award discretionary grants, to give priority to those communities that are making good faith progress toward creating new housing. His order also made $9 million available over the next two years for community planning to help cities and towns find ways to make more housing available while also preserving open space.

- **New Jersey**. The state's successful Rehabilitation Subcode puts a twist on building regulations because it provides clear language for the renovation of existing structures that may not readily fit the mold of new building codes. Developers have embraced the new standards, which make rehabilitation of older buildings more affordable and attractive – spurring urban renewal in cities across the state by as much as 60 percent. Governor Christine Todd Whitman recently demonstrated her support of "smart growth" by canceling a suburban state office project, keeping 900 jobs in Trenton.
- **Delaware.** Governor Thomas Carper reached agreement between the state and each county about where growth should occur and when it should happen. During his Administration, over a quarter-billion dollars have been earmarked for farmland preservation and open space programs.
- **Georgia.** The General Assembly passed Governor Roy Barnes' open-space preservation program. The program offers $30 million to 40 eligible counties willing to develop plans to protect 20 percent of land from development.
- **Maryland.** The General Assembly passed both parts of Governor Parris Glendening's "Smart Codes" proposal. The first part revamps building codes to make it easier to rehabilitate existing structures. The goal is to increase redevelopment in neglected urban areas, help cities and towns rid themselves of rundown or vacant buildings, and give developers less reason to convert farmland and open space into more subdivisions. The second part of Glendening's legislative package directs the development of two model codes for voluntary local adoption. One would encourage infill in existing areas and the other would encourage more 'smart neighborhoods' with compact, mixed-use, transit-oriented development.
- **Ohio.** The General Assembly approved Governor Bob Taft's request for a $400 million bond issue to redevelop brownfields, protect streams, preserve farmland, and establish greenways, bike paths, and other recreational areas. The issue goes before the voters in November 2000.

Forging Regional Partnerships

Many cooperative efforts are aimed at forging regional partnerships to address common problems that cross local boundaries. These broad-based partnerships – including private individuals, businesses, non-profits, foundations, and the government – can encompass many jurisdictions and address a wide variety of issues. While regional approaches are not new, a report by the National Academy of Public Administration (NAPA) identified five broad categories of current challenges that are creating renewed interest in "thinking regionally:"

- **Developing a workforce:** preparing and linking people with jobs in rapidly growing suburbs.

- **Competing economically:** building world class research facilities, transportation systems, and supplier networks.
- **Quality of life:** protecting the environment, controlling traffic congestion and injuries, and preserving safe, healthy communities.
- **Paying for growth:** making wise investments in public facilities in growing suburbs.
- **Redevelopment:** revitalizing inner cities and first tier suburbs.

The number of regional efforts is growing. A survey by the National Association of Regional Councils and NAPA revealed that there are an average of a dozen regional organizations in every part of the nation in the forefront of local efforts to "think regionally."

In some places, citizens across a region are coming together to address the problems that threaten air quality, water quality, and open space. In others, partnerships are forming around economic and social challenges, such as preparing urban youth for high-tech jobs in the outer suburbs. Jurisdictions are joining forces in many cases because they recognize that they cannot effectively meet challenges such as crime and transportation on their own. Not only does one community's decision affect another, but often there are opportunities for cost-sharing, cost reduction, or improved service quality if these issues are jointly addressed.

There is growing awareness of the importance of regional approaches to economic development. A study conducted by Standard and Poor's DRI for the U.S. Conference of Mayors and the National Association of Counties in 1999 found that 317 "metropolitan economic engines" drive the growth which has made America the number one economic nation on earth. These metro economic engines are comprised of core cities, neighboring suburbs, surrounding counties, and the businesses within them, which account for approximately four out of every five Americans. According to the Conference of Mayors, if city/county metro economies were ranked with nations, 47 of the world's top 100 economies would be U.S. metropolitan areas.

The renewed emphasis on "thinking regionally" raises the question of the appropriate role for the federal government in supporting regional cooperation. When considering this issue, the NAPA concluded that:

> **The federal government should lend its support to regional efforts without trying to suggest how regions should frame their goals and opportunities. This would require a light hand, an agile approach, a recognition of diversity – not attributes the federal government is well-known for. So the federal government will have to learn new approaches and new skills if it is to encourage more intelligent approaches to the country's regional problems.**

These new approaches are best exemplified by the projects emerging from the Partnership for Regional Livability. These innovative partnerships demonstrate the promise of regional solutions and represent a better way for the federal government to work with regions (see pages 58-62)

Common Threads

Although local, regional, and state efforts are driven by different needs, rely on different mechanisms, and have different geographic scales, common threads run throughout many of these diverse efforts:

- **Locally-Driven.** These are efforts designed by local people and organizations to solve local problems and take advantage of local assets. They are not responses to federal mandates.
- **Inclusive Partnerships.** Successful partnerships involve everyone with a stake in the future of a community. Such efforts thrive on the active participation of local government, the private sector, the non-profit sector, community-based organizations, faith-based organizations, and individual citizens.
- **Broad Scope.** Successful efforts to create or maintain healthy, livable communities often achieve lasting solutions when economic, equity, and environmental challenges are pursued simultaneously.
- **Resilient Local Economies.** Interest is growing in economic development strategies that seek to create resilient local economies that make unique local assets a source of competitive advantage in the global economy. 
- **Smart Growth.** There is increasing support for the kinds of growth that build on existing investments and avoid economic inefficiency, reduction in quality of life, and environmental damage associated with current patterns of development.
- **Regional in Scale.** Some communities have come to the conclusion that central cities, suburban areas, and surrounding rural communities within a region are interdependent and share a common destiny. A region or metropolitan area may be the best scale to implement economic strategies to build resilient economies; to adopt policies to encourage smarter patterns of growth; to protect open space and parks; and to address equity issues such as crime, traffic injuries and fatalities, reverse commutes, job creation, and housing affordability.
- **Performance-Based.** Local strategies often contain indicators or benchmarks to ensure accountability and to measure progress toward the goals contained in a community-driven strategic plan.
- **Traditional Values.** The success of local efforts depends upon commitment to traditional American values such as cooperation, personal responsibility, equal opportunity, work, and stewardship.

THE FEDERAL ROLE IN BUILDING LIVABLE COMMUNITIES

The emergence of this "wave of local innovation" raises the question of the appropriate role for the federal government in building livable communities. The Clinton-Gore Administration strongly believes that it is the responsibility of the federal government to support, not to try to direct, such efforts. As a result, the Administration's Livable Communities Initiative is based upon three guiding principles:

- **Communities Know Best.** Land use decisions have traditionally been – and must remain – the domain of state and local government. Each community should grow according to its own values. There is no good reason for the federal government to insert itself into these inherently local decisions. Local people know their communities best. The federal government must respect the value of local wisdom.

- **Collaboration Works.** Three types of collaborative partnerships can help build more livable communities:

  Partnerships across sectors, bringing together government, business, and non-governmental organizations;

  Partnerships across local geography, bringing together cities, suburbs, and rural areas in a region to achieve common goals; and

  Partnerships among communities, regions, states, and the federal government to build more livable communities.

- **Reinvention is Imperative.** To be an effective partner in support of local priorities requires a fundamental shift in the way the federal government traditionally operates. This reinvented federal government can support local efforts to build livable communities in three ways:

  Understanding Places. The federal government must be sufficiently flexible and innovative to tailor its policies and programs to meet the unique, locally determined needs of specific places;

  Integrating Policies. The federal government must seek innovative ways to simultaneously achieve economic, social, and environmental policy goals; and

  Coordinating Actions. The federal government must cooperate across agencies so livable communities policies and programs reflect local needs, not the organizational structure of federal agencies.

Building upon these guiding principles, the Clinton-Gore Administration has developed the Livable Communities Initiative. The initiative is a comprehensive 30-point package of policy actions and voluntary partnerships. It is based upon the fundamental assumption that the federal responsibility in building livable communities is to support locally driven efforts by aligning federal resources in support of local priorities. The Livable Communities Initiative focuses on four ways that the federal government can play this supportive role:

- **Expanding Community Choices by Providing Incentives.** The federal government can expand the choices available to communities that wish to pursue livable communities policies by providing financial or regulatory incentives;
- **Expanding Community Choices by Providing Information.** The federal government can expand the choices available to communities by providing information, tools, and technical assistance to enhance local decision-making;
- **Being a Good Neighbor.** The policies of the federal government for managing its buildings, workforce, lands, and facilities should support, not hinder, livable communities efforts in the places the federal government operates; and
- **Building Partnerships.** The federal government can support local livable communities efforts by participating in a variety of collaborative partnerships with communities, regions, the private sector, non-profits, and academic institutions in places across the country.

Consistent with both the guiding principles and these four roles, the Livable Communities Initiative that follows will ensure that the federal government will be an effective partner in support of local efforts to build livable communities in the 21st Century.

THE LIVABLE COMMUNITIES INITIATIVE

The Livable Communities Initiative is a comprehensive 30-point package of policy initiatives and partnerships designed to support locally driven efforts to build more livable communities. The package was developed under the leadership of the White House Task Force on Livable Communities. The Task Force was created by the Clinton-Gore Administration in August 1999 to coordinate livable communities policies and activities across 18 agencies of the executive branch of the federal government. The 30 elements of the Livable Communities Initiative are organized into four categories that represent significant ways the federal government can play a supportive role in building livable communities:

- Expanding Community Choices by Providing Incentives;
- Expanding Community Choices by Providing Information;
- Being a Good Neighbor; and
- Building Partnerships.

Taken together, the programs and activities represented in this 30-point package will support local efforts to sustain prosperity, expand economic opportunity, and improve quality of life in communities and regions across the nation. These actions include:

- Revitalizing existing communities;
- Improving the environment, public health, and quality of life;
- Providing more transportation choices;
- Improving schools and making them centers of communities;
- Expanding economic opportunity;
- Increasing public safety and crime prevention;
- Protecting farmland and open space; and
- Becoming disaster-resistant.

By drawing upon the assets and resources of the federal sector, the Livable Communities Initiative supports state and local smart growth efforts and helps communities chart a new course. America's communities should, and will, continue to grow. Sprawl, however, is not inevitable. By joining together – and drawing on federal tools and resources – citizens can shape future growth to create more livable communities where families can enjoy sustained prosperity, personal freedom, a strong sense of community, and a high quality of life. The Livable Communities Initiative demonstrates the Clinton-Gore Administration's commitment to meeting its responsibilities as a partner in building more livable communities.

EXPANDING COMMUNITY CHOICES BY PROVIDING INCENTIVES

The livability challenges facing communities are as diverse as the communities themselves. Tackling these challenges requires a variety of strategies based on the unique assets and needs of the community. The federal government can support local efforts to address livability issues by expanding the choices available to communities by providing incentives. Such incentives can take a variety of forms. They can be financial incentives to provide resources to communities that choose to protect open space or improve access to mass transit. Or they can be regulatory incentives that provide communities with the opportunity to achieve clean air and clean water goals in a manner consistent with the economic revitalization of older communities.

Better America Bonds

ISSUE: Across America, communities are searching for ways to keep growing while preserving a high quality of life. In the 1998 elections, 240 "green" ballot initiatives were considered in communities across the country. More than 70 percent of these measures to protect open space and enhance local livability were adopted, authorizing $7.5 billion in state and local spending. Last fall, 25 states approved 90 percent of open space ballot initiatives, authorizing approximately $2 billion – a total of more than $9 billion in bonding authority to state and local communities in the last two elections. These communities were responding, in part, to the loss of open space that has occurred across the nation. The federal government can expand the choices available to communities that wish to address this problem by helping finance the revitalization of older neighborhoods, improving water quality, and protecting green space and farmland close to home.

ACTION: The centerpiece of the Livable Communities Initiative is a proposal to create a new financing tool for communities called Better America Bonds. At a cost of approximately $700 million over five years, Better America Bonds will enable state, local, and tribal governments to issue $10.75 billion of tax credit bonds over five years. Communities will have access to zero interest financing because investors buying these fifteen-year bonds will receive tax credits in lieu of interest.

Better America Bonds offer a creative way for states and communities to preserve and enhance open space, create or restore parks, clean up brownfields, protect threatened farmland and wetlands, and improve water quality. Local communities can partner with land trust groups, business leaders, environmentalists, and others to implement creative and innovative solutions to their community's development challenges.

This is not a big government program. The federal government will not purchase one square inch of land. Nor will it micromanage local zoning and land use decisions. States and communities will build their own legacy. All decisions will be made at the state or local level. Through Better America Bonds, the federal government will expand the choices available to communities by providing them with a vital new tool they can use to grow in ways that are best for them. More information is available at <www.epa.gov/bonds>.

Expanding Community Transportation Choices

ISSUE: As communities grow farther out and commuting distances increase, more and more Americans find themselves sitting in traffic. The Department of Transportation calculates that 41 percent of peak-hour traffic is under congested conditions. As a result, metropolitan areas in the United States are experiencing unprecedented challenges to mobility. In the past decade alone, metropolitan traffic grew by 30 percent, resulting in chronic gridlock. The two billion hours Americans spend stuck in traffic every year results in more than $48 billion in lost productivity. An analysis by the Surface Transportation Policy Project found that 69 percent of the increased driving from 1983 to 1990 was due to factors influenced by sprawl. The actions that follow represent a comprehensive package of incentives using the federal budget, the tax code, credit programs, and investments in technology to expand the transportation choices available to communities.

ACTION: TRANSPORTATION ALTERNATIVES

The Administration's budget submission includes a record $9.1 billion to help reduce traffic congestion, pollution, and oil consumption – a $1.1 billion increase over last year's funding level. The budget includes the following elements to expand community transportation choices that enhance mobility, economic competitiveness, and quality of life.

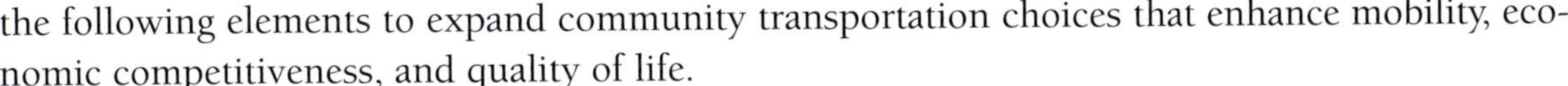

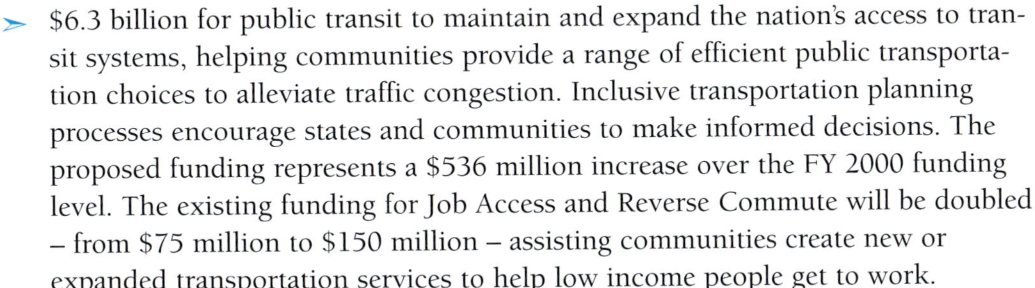

- $6.3 billion for public transit to maintain and expand the nation's access to transit systems, helping communities provide a range of efficient public transportation choices to alleviate traffic congestion. Inclusive transportation planning processes encourage states and communities to make informed decisions. The proposed funding represents a $536 million increase over the FY 2000 funding level. The existing funding for Job Access and Reverse Commute will be doubled – from $75 million to $150 million – assisting communities create new or expanded transportation services to help low income people get to work.
- $1.6 billion for the Congestion Mitigation and Air Quality Improvement Program will support state and local efforts to simultaneously ease congestion and reduce air pollution in areas not meeting or working to stay in compliance with federal air quality standards. Eligible projects include high occupancy vehicle lanes, incentives for ridesharing, improved transit facilities, systems to monitor traffic and quickly clear disabled vehicles, bicycle and pedestrian paths, and conversion of public and private fleets to cleaner fuels. The proposed funding represents a $47 million increase over the FY 2000 funding level.
- $719 million for the Transportation Enhancements Program to support projects such as the renovation of historic rail stations, creation of bicycle and pedestrian

paths, safety education, and scenic beautification. The proposed funding represents a $34 million increase over the FY 2000 funding level.

- $468 million for the Expanded Passenger Rail Fund to support the continued development of a vibrant passenger rail system in this country. The fund would be administered by the Secretary of Transportation with funds allocated to Amtrak and the states. Under this program, Amtrak would be required to partner with states on rail corridor improvements. Eligible capital projects include acquisition of equipment and construction of infrastructure improvements, including securing of rights-of-way.

- $52 million for the Transportation and Community and System Preservation Pilot, to provide grants to state and local governments and planning agencies to coordinate transportation and land use planning while reducing environmental impacts and ensuring efficient access to jobs, services and centers of trade. The proposed funding represents a $17 million increase over the FY 2000 funding level.

ACTION: NEW TRANSIT STARTS

The transportation budget includes funding for New Starts, the federal government's primary financial resource for supporting locally planned, implemented, and operated transit "fixed guideway" capital investments. From heavy to light rail, from commuter rail to bus rapid transit systems, the New Starts program has helped make possible hundreds of new or extended transit fixed guideway systems across the country. These rail and bus investments have, in turn, improved the mobility of millions of Americans, helped to reduce congestion and improve air quality in the areas they serve, and fostered the development of economically viable, safer, and more livable communities.

In the Transportation Equity Act for the 21st Century (TEA-21), Congress reaffirmed support for the Department of Transportation's Federal Transit Administration's (FTA) evaluation and rating of proposed New Start projects, including new land use criteria, to ensure that the $6 billion provided for new transit systems under TEA-21 will be invested in ways that help communities grow smarter. Criteria for New Starts project selection now include:

- Existing land use;
- Containment of sprawl;
- Transit-supportive corridor practices;
- Supportive zoning regulations near transit; and
- Tools to implement land use policies and gauge the performance of those policies.

The President's FY 2001 Budget proposes continued funding for 14 fixed guideway transit projects currently under construction, and commitments to build 15 new systems.

ACTION: INNOVATIVE FINANCE TO SPUR TRANSPORTATION INVESTMENT

The federal government cannot afford to fund every transportation investment necessary to make our communities more livable. But federal credit programs can help leverage non-federal investment. The Transportation Infrastructure Finance and Innovation Act of 1998 (TIFIA) provides federal credit assistance to major transportation investments of critical national and regional importance. The TIFIA program provides direct loans, loan guarantees, and lines of credit and is designed to fill market gaps and leverage private co-investment by providing supplemental and subordinate capital. A total of $530 million in federal funding is provided to pay the "subsidy cost" of supporting federal credit under TIFIA. Annual caps totaling $10.6 billion limit the principal amount of credit instruments issued. Any project eligible for federal assistance through existing surface transportation programs (highway projects and transit capital projects) is eligible for the TIFIA credit program. Intercity passenger bus and rail facilities and vehicles and publicly owned intermodal freight facilities are also eligible. The first round of TIFIA projects in FY 1999 provided $1.6 billion of credit assistance to projects in California, the District of Columbia, Florida, New York, and Puerto Rico. This credit assistance supported $6.5 billion in intermodal and transit projects, at a cost to the federal government of only $61 million.

ACTION: COMMUTER CHOICE INITIATIVE

Federal law allows employers to offer tax incentives to their employees to encourage a variety of means for getting to work. Commuter Choice employee benefit packages save money for businesses and employees by offering workers incentives for transit, vanpooling, carpooling, teleworking, biking, and walking. Some states offer additional Commuter Choice tax breaks for employees to take transit, vanpool, or give up their parking spot at work.

The Federal Coalition for Commuter Choice is developing a strategic plan to assist communities with implementing comprehensive Commuter Choice Initiatives with businesses in their areas. The Coalition includes representatives from the Environmental Protection Agency (EPA); the Departments of Transportation, Labor, Health and Human Services, and Energy; the Office of Personnel Management; and the General Services Administration. Other partners include the American Management Association, Environmental Defense, and the Alliance for Clean Air and Transportation. These partners have provided nearly $1 million to implement the Commuter Choice Initiative. Actions include:

- Development of a comprehensive web site: <COMMUTERCHOICE.COM>;
- Development of Commuter Choice training sessions for the private sector;
- Design, distribution, and support for EPA's user-friendly, PC-based quantification tool; and
- Provision of in-depth supporting information to the public, employers, and communities.

The goal of the Commuter Choice Initiative is for all employers across the nation to offer Commuter Choice employee benefit packages by 2005.

ACTION: INTELLIGENT TRANSPORTATION SYSTEMS

Communities can alleviate congestion by making more efficient use of their existing infrastructure through the application of Intelligent Transportation Systems (ITS). Such technologies include:

- Freeway management systems to provide information to motorists, detect capacity and flow problems, and minimize congestion from crashes.
- Regional multimodal traveler information systems to provide road and transit information to travelers, businesses, and motor carriers, so they can adjust travel plans when necessary.
- Transit management systems to allow new ways of monitoring and maintaining transit fleets through advanced locating devices and equipment-monitoring systems.
- Electronic fare payment systems to enable a person to pay for parking, tolls, and bus and train fares by using a single smart card.
- Electronic toll collection to provide both drivers and transportation agencies with convenient and reliable automated transactions, dramatically improving traffic flow at toll plazas and increasing the operational efficiency of toll collecting.
- Emergency response coordination to ensure the closest available and most appropriate emergency unit can be dispatched to a crash.
- Incident management programs to enable communities to identify and respond to crashes or breakdowns with the best and quickest type of emergency services, minimizing clean-up and medical response time.
- Traffic signal control systems that automatically adjust to optimize traffic flow.
- Railroad crossings coordinated with traffic signals and train movements.

The federal government invests in the development of ITS technology to give states and local governments the option of investing their federal transportation funds in the deployment of ITS as a means of relieving traffic congestion.

Reclaiming Brownfields

ISSUE: Brownfields are abandoned or underutilized properties on which redevelopment is complicated by real or perceived industrial contamination. Over 200 cities responded to a recent U.S. Conference of Mayors survey by reporting more than 21,000 brownfields sites covering some 125,000 acres – an area equal to Boston, Minneapolis, Pittsburgh, and San Francisco combined. The Mayors survey indicated that redeveloping these brownfields would realize $878 million to $2.4 billion in increased tax revenues, generate more than 550,000 jobs, and could support another 5.8 million people without adding appreciably to local infrastructure. Redeveloping brownfields is critical to revitalizing our cities, bringing good jobs to blighted communities, and reducing pressures for greenfields development. More information is available at <www.epa.gov/brownfields>.

ACTION: BROWNFIELDS LEGISLATION

The Administration supports brownfields legislation that encourages the cleanup and development of brownfields. Any brownfields legislation must:

- Provide appropriate liability protection for prospective purchasers, contiguous property owners, and truly innocent land owners;

- Provide adequate funding and authority for assessment and cleanup;
- Make permanent the current brownfields tax incentives; and
- Preserve critical safeguards to protect the public health of communities.

ACTION: BROWNFIELDS ECONOMIC REDEVELOPMENT INITIATIVE

The Administration will expand its successful brownfields program to bring the environmental, economic, and community benefits of cleanup and redevelopment to more cities and towns across the country. To date, federal brownfields programs have assessed 1,933 brownfields properties, created more than 5,800 jobs, and leveraged more than $2.3 billion in cleanup and redevelopment funds. These programs have resulted in the cleanup of 116 sites, redevelopment of 151 properties, and a determination that 590 sites did not need additional cleanup. In addition, the Administration's program helps other levels of government, communities, and citizens to build the capacity to implement effective brownfields programs of their own, which will facilitate the cleanup and redevelopment of hundreds, and eventually thousands, of sites.

The Brownfields Economic Redevelopment Initiative includes:

- **The Brownfields National Partnership.** More than 20 federal agencies collaborate to provide financial and technical support for brownfields cleanup. To date the partners estimate spending more than $400 million for brownfields work with another $141 million in loan guarantees. For example, the Economic Development Administration's (EDA) brownfields redevelopment grants more than doubled from 1997 to 1998. EDA provided nearly $80 million to 78 brownfield projects, including planning, technical assistance, public works, and base closure projects. A centerpiece of the partnership is the designation of 16 Brownfields Showcase Communities in 1998. This year, the federal partners plan to designate 10 new Showcase Communities, and have included livability criteria as part of the selection process.

- **Brownfields Assessment Demonstration Pilots.** Since 1994, the Environmental Protection Agency (EPA) has awarded 307 brownfields site assessment demonstration pilots (up to $200,000 each). In FY 2000, EPA will fund 50 new site assessment grants and supplement up to 50 existing pilots. Combined with EPA's property assessment efforts, these pilots identify the extent of contamination, estimate cleanup costs, and develop cleanup plans. EPA has requested funding in FY 2001 to support additional assessment pilots.

- **Brownfields Cleanup Revolving Loan Funds.** These funds allow states, tribes, and localities to capitalize cleanup funds. To date, EPA has awarded 68 grants representing 88 communities. For FY 2000, EPA is reviewing applications from 60 communities and has requested funding in FY 2001 to support these grants.
- **Brownfields Job Training and Development Demonstration Pilots.** Since 1998 EPA has awarded 21 pilots for job training programs located within or near brownfields communities. In FY 2000, EPA will award up to $200,000 each to 10 more pilots.
- **HUD's Brownfields Economic Development Initiative.** This Department of Housing and Urban Development initiative makes competitive grants to cities in combination with Section 108 loan guarantees to help them rehabilitate or redevelop contaminated sites, thereby creating jobs. The FY 2001 Budget proposes a major acceleration of the initiative, doubling program funding from the $25 million enacted in FY 2000 to $50 million in FY 2001.
- **State Voluntary Cleanup Programs.** Through its pilots and partnerships, the Administration continues to empower other governments, communities, and citizens to assess, cleanup, and redevelop brownfields. To date, EPA has signed agreements with 14 states to facilitate the cleanup of contaminated sites that pose lower risks than those EPA typically cleans up under the Superfund program. In FY 2000, EPA is providing states with $10 million to support the development and enhancement of State Voluntary Cleanup programs and has requested funding in FY 2001 to provide further support.

ACTION: USING COMMUNITY DEVELOPMENT BLOCK GRANTS TO CLEAN UP BROWNFIELDS

The Department of Housing and Urban Development will revise the "Prevent or Eliminate Slums or Blight" national objective under its Community Development Block Grant (CDBG) program to recognize explicitly that economic disinvestment and environmental contamination are blighting influences. This change will make it clear that states and localities can spend CDBG funds on assessing and cleaning up brownfields.

ACTION: BROWNFIELDS TO BRIGHTFIELDS

The Department of Energy is working with private industry to encourage the construction and use of clean energy factories and generation facilities on brownfields sites. This innovative program is being piloted in Boston, Chicago, and possibly San Diego. Clean energy manufacturing and generation can facilitate job creation and economic development, and help communities clean their air.

ACTION: RESOURCE CONSERVATION AND RECOVERY ACT BROWNFIELDS PREVENTION INITIATIVE

The Environmental Protection Agency selected pilot projects to help showcase reforms under the Resource Conservation and Recovery Act to make it easier to cleanup and reuse these sites. The four pilots chosen are: Bethlehem Steel Corp., Lackawanna, New York; Blue Valley Redevelopment Team, Kansas City, Missouri; Philadelphia Electric Company, Chester, Pennsylvania; and CBS, Bridgeport, Connecticut.

School Modernization and Construction

ISSUE: The quality of our communities' public schools has a direct bearing on the vitality and livability of our neighborhoods. The General Accounting Office estimates that $112 billion is needed to bring America's existing school facilities into good overall condition. Another recent report found that the average public school in America is 42 years old – school buildings begin rapid deterioration after 40 years. In addition, it is estimated that 2,400 new public schools will be needed by 2003 to accommodate rising enrollments and relieve overcrowding.

ACTION: The School Modernization Proposal contained in the President's FY 2001 Budget advocates two school modernization initiatives to help repair and renovate existing schools and build new ones. In addition, states will continue to have access to flexible bonding authority to finance school renovation and repairs.

- The budget proposes a $1.3 billion school emergency loan and grant initiative. This new funding will leverage nearly $7 billion for urgently needed renovations in high-need school districts. Over five years, the program would leverage $33.5 billion, enough to help as many as 25,000 schools.
- The budget also includes the President's School Modernization Bonds proposal. This proposal will cost $2.4 billion over five years and will leverage $24.8 billion in tax credit bonds to support the construction or modernization of 6,000 schools.
- States also have the option to use Qualified Zone Academy Bonds (QZABs), a relatively new financing instrument to support needed school renovations and repairs. The federal government covers, on average, all of the interest on these bonds, enabling schools to save up to 50 percent of construction project costs. The interest payment is actually a tax credit, in lieu of cash, provided to financial institutions that hold the bonds. Congress, in the last four years, has made a total of $1.2 billion in QZAB bonding authority available to all states. An additional $400 million will be allocated in 2001. Over 20 states have already distributed, or are in the processing of distributing, at least part of their allocations to their districts, and another five are actively planning implementation of the QZAB program.

Using Open Space to Enhance Communities

ISSUE: Studies increasingly demonstrate what communities know instinctively: open space is important to our quality of life. An adequate level and configuration of open space, or "green infrastructure," is as important to urban, suburban, and rural communities as other elements of their community infrastructure. Proximity to parks, farm and forest land, and other natural areas are factors many people consider when locating or purchasing a home or business because open space increases property values, while providing environmental benefits and recreational opportunities.

Investing in community parks and greenways is one way to improve the quality of urban life and reinforce older neighborhoods as good places to live and do business. Parks and other green infrastructure enhance property values and contribute to the economic and social stability of neighborhoods. Community parks provide places for communities to come together, for people to exercise or relax, and for children and adults to play. But parks are more than an amenity – they are an essential component of community life, producing measurable health, social, and economic benefits. Public investment in parks and open space invigorates community revitalization. Economically, parks increase property values, reduce health care costs, improve productivity, and stimulate the type of growth that leads to tourism. This in turn can make cities more appealing as places to live and work while reducing the pressure to develop greenfields on the city's fringe.

Many communities also want to maintain agriculture and forestry in rapidly growing areas to contribute to the local economy and provide aesthetic and environmental benefits to the community. Agricultural and forest lands support jobs on and off the farm. Properly managed, they also help improve water quality, protect wetlands and wildlife habitat, control runoff, filter pollutants from the air and water, and reduce noise pollution. Some of the nation's most productive land lies within rapidly growing regions. In fact, more than half of U.S. agricultural output, including three-fourths of our domestic fruits and vegetables, comes from lands located near urban or suburban centers. However, high land values, land fragmentation, environmental pressures, and other factors make it difficult for many producers to continue farming where there is rapid development.

Preliminary Department of Agriculture data show the conversion of forest, cropland, and open land to urban and other uses increased significantly between 1992 and 1997, confirming that traditional suburban development patterns have accelerated. This loss of open space affects communities in several ways, and many now seek to protect open space to preserve or enhance their quality of life.

ACTION: THE LANDS LEGACY INITIATIVE

The President's Lands Legacy Initiative dedicates nearly $600 million to state and local governments, private land trusts, and other nonprofit groups to help communities protect local green spaces, improve air and water quality, sustain wildlife, and provide families with places to play and relax. These funds will help communities save parks from being paved over and farms from being turned into strip malls. Communities will be able to acquire new lands for urban and suburban forests and recreation sites and set aside new wetlands, coastal and wildlife preserves. Lands Legacy imposes no green mandates and no red tape. Instead, it gives communities the resources they need to make the most of their own possibilities. Funding is proposed for the following programs, which are designed to complement the new bonding authority proposed under the Better America Bonds initiative:

- **Land Acquisition Grants.** $150 million in matching grants for acquisitions of land or easements for urban parks, greenways, outdoor recreation, wetlands, and wildlife habitat.
- **Open Space Planning Grants and Loans.** $50 million in matching grants for open space planning to help communities develop "smart growth" plans for open space preservation and strategies to manage urban growth, and an additional $6 million for a new revolving loan program to support acquisition of land easements in rural areas by rural businesses, land trusts, and other nonprofit organizations.
- **Urban Parks and Forests.** $40 million to establish, maintain, and expand urban and community forests, and $20 million to restore parks in distressed urban neighborhoods.
- **Farmland Protection.** $65 million for matching grants to help states and local communities protect farmland threatened by development.
- **Forest and Wetlands Protection.** $60 million to buy conservation easements on private forest land threatened by development, and $30 million for matching grants to protect and restore wetlands.

- **Non-game Wildlife Habitat Protection.** $100 million to help states protect non-game wildlife by acquiring, protecting, and enhancing critical habitat for wildlife, and $65 million to support habitat conservation plans.
- **Coasts and Oceans.** $265 million to help coastal communities protect and preserve coastal resources.

ACTION: COMMUNITY PARKS INITIATIVE

The federal government has a number of funding and technical assistance programs designed to address the need for parks and recreation, but these programs are not sufficiently coordinated across departments and do not effectively leverage government and non-governmental resources. The Departments of Agriculture (USDA) and Interior (DOI) will assist community organizations and local governments interested in capitalizing on investments in community parks by:

- Coordinating the two programs that directly affect urban park development – USDA's Urban and Community Forestry (UC&F) Program and DOI's Urban Park and Recreation Recovery (UPARR) Program. UC&F provides matching grants to states and communities to establish, maintain, and expand urban and community forests and related green spaces, such as parks, gardens, and greenways. UPARR provides matching grants and technical assistance for the restoration of parks in economically distressed urban communities. The complementary nature of these two programs provides the foundation for USDA and DOI to build a comprehensive approach to community parks issues that includes other federal agencies and non-federal partners willing to provide matching dollars to leverage program funds.

- Developing a complete toolbox of funding resources and technical assistance.
- Targeting technical assistance and funding opportunities across agencies to help city and suburban neighborhoods address their park and recreation needs.
- Working with several agencies, including the Environmental Protection Agency, the National Endowment for the Arts, the U.S. Army Corps of Engineers, and the Departments of Housing and Urban Development, Transportation, Justice, and Defense, to better integrate community parks into larger planning and design processes. These activities will relate to reclaiming brownfields, redeveloping military bases, preserving rail corridors, improving transportation, developing housing, encouraging economic development, preventing flood damage, performing environmental restoration, and using design to increase community involvement.
- Exploring opportunities to leverage federal funds under the UPARR and U&CF programs with matching dollars from foundations and corporations, as well as with existing federal programs such as Community Development Block Grants.

ACTION: MAINTAINING AGRICULTURE AND FORESTRY IN RAPIDLY GROWING AREAS

The Department of Agriculture will establish a new task force to identify actions to help maintain agriculture and forestry in rapidly growing regions. This task force will oversee a study to assess the economic, environmental, and social demands that rapidly developing areas place on our farms, forest lands, and other natural resources. The task force may recommend ways the federal government can better serve private farmers and forest operators and help them deal with land fragmentation, high land costs, and environmental demands, and take advantage of unique opportunities such as direct marketing and agri-tourism. It also will consider the extent to which actions by federal agencies, such as construction, development grants and loans, and federal land management decisions, contribute to the loss of farm and forest lands and whether additional measures or policy changes can be taken to lessen their impact. The task force will conduct public forums across the country and report its findings and recommendations to the Secretary of Agriculture at a special workshop devoted to these issues.

ACTION: MILLENNIUM GARDENS

An essential element of any community's green infrastructure is its gardens. The USDA Millennium Gardens Initiative develops public/private partnerships to increase community and school gardens and to provide excess food for organizations that help feed low-income Americans. To reach the goal, the Department and its partners in the Cooperative Extension System will provide technical assistance and, in some instances, seed money for such efforts. In addition, the President's Budget asks Congress to provide $5.25 million in new funding for nonprofit groups and faith-based organizations to expand community-based efforts to fight hunger, improve nutrition, strengthen local food systems, and help low-income families move from poverty to self-sufficiency.

Expanding Opportunities for Affordable Housing

ISSUE: The federal government can provide incentives to encourage affordable single family, multi-family, and rental housing. Affordable housing is necessary for the development of sustainable, livable communities.

ACTION: NEIGHBORHOOD REINVESTMENT CORPORATION

A contributing factor to declining neighborhoods is the lack of resources available for community investment and affordable housing. The ability to purchase and own a home empowers individuals and families and enables them to invest in their communities. Organizations that leverage public and private resources and create affordable housing – by raising equity capital and providing technical assistance and training – are critical to the revitalization of our nation's communities.

The Neighborhood Reinvestment Corporation (NRC) is a congressionally chartered non-profit organization operating with federal support. Through its mobilization of private, public, and community resources, and its NeighborWorks® system, the NRC provides an innovative structure for strengthening distressed communities. Nationally, over 200 NeighborWorks® organizations serve more than 1,000 urban, suburban, and rural communities.

Each nonprofit NeighborWorks® organization, locally governed by residents and community leaders, raises its own funds and sets strategies for community revitalization and growth through the use of a revolving loan fund. Revolving loan funds are locally controlled investment pools, supported by grants and loans from the NRC, government, businesses, and foundations. NeighborWorks® makes loans, considered risky in the conventional market, to target neighborhoods from the revolving loan fund. The Neighborhood Housing Services of America (NHSA) then purchases these loans in order to replenish the investment pool. These purchases provide a consistent stream of capital into NeighborWorks® organizations, enabling these organizations to serve their communities.

In FY 2001, NRC will continue to invest in local, flexible revolving loan funds and work with partners on a national level to help local organizations increase other direct investment to preserve both single family and multifamily affordable housing. It will focus its efforts on helping NeighborWorks® organizations construct new and rehabilitate existing housing, create mutual housing associations, develop revitalization strategies, and acquire problem properties or properties in the process of disposition. Revolving loan investments and capital investments are projected to total $103 million and other direct investments are projected to total $1.2 billion.

ACTION: MAINTAINING AFFORDABLE RURAL RENTAL HOUSING

Many rural communities suffer from a tremendous shortage of affordable rental housing. USDA's Rural Housing Service has funded more than 18,000 multi-family rental complexes, which provide decent, safe, and affordable homes to more than 450,000 people in rural America. Many of these complexes are aging and in need of repair. To help communities preserve this valuable housing stock, USDA is dedicating approximately 40 percent of its Section 515 rural rental housing loan funds to repair and rehabilitate these homes. Preserving existing rural housing stock usually costs less than new construction, improves area property values, and maintains community stability. Most importantly, it ensures that tenants continue to live in high quality, affordable housing.

Crime-Solving Initiatives to Improve Community Safety

ISSUE: Ensuring public safety is an essential element of building livable communities. The Administration has already funded over 100,000 additional police officers on the street and proposes to fund up to an additional 50,000. In addition to increased police presence on the street, state and local law enforcement should be equipped with effective crime-solving technologies to improve our law enforcement officials' ability to protect public safety.

ACTION: THE ADMINISTRATION'S FY 2001 BUDGET ALLOCATES RESOURCES TO:

- **Facilitate the Exchange of Criminal History Records.** The FY 2001 Budget will provide $70 million for states to improve the quality and immediate accessibility of criminal history records and ensure that offenders cannot escape the efforts of police between states due to gaps in technology. These funds will also assist states in integrating their systems with those operated by the Justice Department's Federal Bureau of Investigation (FBI). This integration will help facilitate presale checks on prospective handgun purchasers and employment checks on child and elder care workers, as well as ensure that the most accurate information is available for the National Sex Offender Registry;

- **Improve the Capabilities of State and Local Crime Labs.** The FY 2001 Budget provides $35 million in grants to state and local government agencies to improve their investigative and analytical capabilities in forensic science. Funding will also provide research, technical assistance, and training to help inform agencies about what lab capabilities are available nationwide and to provide guidance on what types of equipment to purchase. Of this total, $5 million is targeted to Indian Tribes.

- **Reduce the DNA Sample Backlog.** To reduce the DNA sample backlog of one million convicted offenders at state and local crime labs, $15 million has been requested. Reducing this backlog will enable law enforcement to match crime scene DNA to the FBI's national database (CODIS) more effectively. The budget includes an additional $5 million to develop technology tools that make DNA testing faster, cheaper, and better.

- **Transfer Federal Technologies to Localities.** The Office of National Drug Control Policy (ONDCP) has requested approximately $20 million for continuation of its Counterdrug Technology Assessment Center's (CTAC) Technology Transfer Program. CTAC sponsors programs to develop advanced technology to improve drug-related law enforcement capabilities. Federally developed technology, such as wireless communications equipment, night-vision equipment, automated law enforcement case management tools, and drug detection devices, are available to state and local law enforcement agencies through the Technology

Transfer Program. To date, over 1,200 law enforcement agencies have received such equipment and systems.

- **Building Blocks Initiative.** The FY 2001 Budget requests funding to implement proven delinquency and crime fighting strategies in 25 jurisdictions across the country. The Building Blocks Initiative will fund the integration of community and state problem-solving capacities, including data mapping street crime, community risk and protective factor assessment, and resource, management, and systems analysis.
- **COMPASS: Community Mapping Planning and Analysis for Safety Strategies**. The FY 2001 Budget requests funding to build local crime data collection and analysis capacity in urban, suburban, and rural communities, and to improve models for predicting crime in neighborhoods. These models will use advanced crime mapping techniques and test the effectiveness of selected community crime prevention interventions. This initiative will provide a comprehensive approach to understanding crime in its local context, and will provide practitioners with the tools needed to adapt to changing crime patterns.
- **SACSI: Strategic Approaches to Community Safety Initiative.** The FY 2001 Budget requests funding to implement a collaborative, information-driven approach to crime reduction in 50 communities across the country. The SACSI model partners federal, state, and local law enforcement, researchers, criminal justice personnel, elected officials, and community members to examine and overcome a targeted crime problem. Preliminary results in Indianapolis, where implementation has been underway the longest, suggest a significant drop in their target crime of homicide. The Office of Justice Programs proposes to implement the initiative in up to 10 new sites every year for the next five years.
- **Build Local Crime Data Collection and Analysis Capacity**. The FY 2001 Budget requests funding to help law enforcement agencies conduct resource, management, and system analysis, and implement technologies such as advanced crime mapping techniques to track and predict crime in neighborhoods. Funding will also help communities develop or improve computer models to test the effectiveness of selected crime prevention interventions. By helping communities use technology to track street crime and assess risk and protective factors, law enforcement will be better prepared to respond to changing crime patterns.

Using the Clean Air Act to Encourage Infill Development

ISSUE: The need to comply with national air quality standards can present localities and states with difficult development decisions. The Clean Air Act can recognize the benefits of infill development without adversely affecting air quality or a locality's compliance.

ACTION: RECOGNIZING THE AIR QUALITY BENEFITS OF LAND USE POLICIES AND PROJECTS

The Environmental Protection Agency (EPA) will issue guidance in the summer of 2000 to support communities that have adopted voluntary land use policies and projects with associated air quality

benefits. These practices promote reduced reliance on automobile travel and reduced emissions of air pollutants. Examples include infill development, improvement and investments in transit systems, removal of density caps, and smart growth development patterns. The guidance will help states and cities recognize and quantify the transportation-related emissions reductions resulting from these policies and projects, and will provide multiple options to recognize the benefits from the adoption of these practices. States and localities can receive credit under the Clean Air Act for these practices, demonstrating that smart growth can have air quality benefits.

ACTION: CLEAN AIR ACT FLEXIBILITY FOR "TARGETED ECONOMIC DEVELOPMENT"

EPA, in consultation with the Department of Housing and Urban Development, has the authority to designate areas "targeted for economic development" (e.g. an Empowerment Zone) in cities that do not meet air quality standards. EPA may grant cities and states more flexibility in demonstrating that new development is consistent with attaining air quality goals. This provision of the Clean Air Act (Section 173) has not yet been implemented, but EPA will pilot the program in Chicago this year. The pilot will demonstrate how the Clean Air Act can encourage infill development, economic empowerment, and the protection of air quality. If the pilot is successful, it will be expanded nationally.

ACTION: CLEAN AIR/BROWNFIELDS PARTNERSHIP PILOTS

EPA and the Economic Development Administration, in conjunction with the U.S. Conference of Mayors, are funding three pilots in Baltimore, Chicago, and Dallas that are contributing to the development of the aforementioned Clean Air Act flexibility programs. Among other things, these pilots are quantifying the air quality and economic benefits of redeveloping brownfields within a city and inner-ring suburbs instead of outlying greenfields. The results will help communities take credit for emissions reductions associated with their redevelopment projects.

ACTION: INTEGRATING ENERGY EFFICIENCY AND RENEWABLE ENERGY INTO CLEAN AIR OBJECTIVES

The Department of Energy and EPA are working with the Environmental Commissioners of States, the National Association of State Energy Offices, and the National Association of Regulatory Utility Commissioners to develop blueprints for states and communities to use energy efficiency and renewable energy to meet air quality objectives in the least costly, most effective way possible. These blueprints will ensure that energy, environmental, and utility restructuring policies are supportive of state and community quality of life goals.

Fostering Livability through Disaster Resistance

ISSUE: Few communities recognize the opportunities available to them to become more disaster-resistant prior to a natural disaster.

ACTION: The Federal Emergency Management Agency (FEMA) launched Project Impact, a nationwide initiative that focuses hazard mitigation assistance directly on communities. Under

Project Impact, communities use FEMA funds as "seed money" to leverage and attract an array of partners to develop community-based disaster resistance strategies. Currently, efforts are underway in 185 communities to reach out to a broad spectrum of businesses, non-profit organizations, government agencies, and local citizens to promote awareness of disaster risks. Communities use that knowledge to create disaster-resistant homes, businesses and communities. This investment strengthens local economies and creates a stronger social and physical environment that is resilient to disaster events.

The benefits of creating a disaster-resistant community are clear. An additional, indirect benefit of Project Impact is that communities learn how to create a proactive and inclusive local decision-making process. As communities develop plans and initiatives to protect lives and property from the devastating effects of a disaster, they engage a broad spectrum of citizens and organizations. By doing this, a strong foundation for consensus forms, which communities can use to work through other, often more contentious, local issues. As a result, Project Impact is improving the local civic capacity not only to help communities become disaster-resistant, but to transform them into healthy places that are livable and sustainable for the long-term.

Incentives for Local Collaboration

ISSUE: The federal government can provide incentives to encourage collaboration on livable communities issues at the local level, across jurisdictional lines, and among a variety of stakeholders.

ACTION: REGIONAL CONNECTIONS

The continued outward expansion of our metropolitan areas makes it increasingly difficult for any single community to effectively address issues that know no local jurisdictional boundaries. These issues include concentrated poverty, housing affordability, transportation, environmental protection, education, and regional economic growth. Communities that cooperate with one another to tackle cross-jurisdictional issues can improve both their own futures and the future of their regions. Increasingly, regions are the economic engines of our national economy and are critical to maintaining our competitive edge in the global marketplace.

The Administration's FY 2001 Budget includes $25 million to fund the Department of Housing and Urban Development's proposed Regional Connections Initiative. The program will promote regional "smart growth" strategies and complement the Administration's other regional efforts. Matching grants will help partnerships of local jurisdictions and states design and pursue smarter growth strategies across jurisdictional lines. Legislation to authorize this program was introduced in Congress.

ACTION: INNOVATIVE COMMUNITY PARTNERSHIP GRANTS

The Environmental Protection Agency (EPA) has created a community grant program, the new Innovative Community Partnership (ICP) grants initiative. Overall funding for the ICP has been proposed in the President's FY 2001 Budget at $4.4 million. EPA will be working with stakeholders over the summer on the final design of its grant criteria and application process and plans to launch the full initiative by early next year. The Agency expects to give priority consideration to ICP project proposals in the following areas:

- Restoration and protection of community watersheds and airsheds;
- Integrated community planning for environmental results; and
- Environmentally responsible redevelopment and revitalization.

As a demonstration, in May 2000, EPA selected 11 innovative community projects for funding as pilots for the new Innovative Community Partnership grants initiative. The individual projects range from community consensus-building in Concord, New Hampshire, to promoting alternatives to sprawl through working partnerships between Silicon Valley businesses and local government. Collectively, they share an emphasis on local innovation, cross-media environmental approaches, and community partnerships to achieve measurable environmental results and promote more livable communities. As part of an interactive partnership process, pilot grant recipients will provide feedback to EPA as they make progress and achieve results.

Assisting Communities with Their Water Needs

ISSUE: The United States historically approached water problems as distinct engineering challenges, often resulting in environmental impacts to communities above and beyond the projects in question. This piecemeal approach to water supply and quality issues often caused an inefficient use of local, state, and federal resources and hampered efforts to deal with watershed problems that transcend political boundaries. Additionally, federal water regulations and grant and loan programs do not always encourage communities to employ innovative strategies to address their needs in a more environmentally sustainable manner.

ACTION: WATER RESOURCE ASSESSMENTS

The U.S. Army Corps of Engineers (USACE), as part of the proposed Water Resources Development Act of 2000, and in cooperation with other federal agencies, will develop assessments of water resource needs in river basins and watersheds in collaboration with state, local, and tribal governments. Such assessments include an evaluation of ecosystem protection and restoration, flood damage reduction, navigation and port needs, watershed protection, water supplies, and drought preparedness. The USACE has requested $15 million to carry out these assessments, with a non-federal cost share of 25 percent.

ACTION: LISTENING SESSIONS

The USACE, in an effort to understand the nature and scope of community water resource needs more fully, is conducting a series of "listening sessions" across the country between June and October 2000. The purpose of these sessions is to encourage a dialogue among stakeholders to assess the needs and priorities for water resources in the nation's future, resulting in a report assessing the current state of water resources and the gap that must be closed to meet future water needs.

ACTION: ASSISTING TRIBES

The USACE has proposed legislation in the Water Resources Development Act of 2000 to provide cost share assistance to federally recognized Indian Tribes to study and determine the feasibility of implementing environmentally sound water resource development projects that will substantially benefit Indian Tribes. Studies will address flood damage reduction, environmental restoration and protection, and preservation of cultural and natural resources.

EXPANDING COMMUNITY CHOICES BY PROVIDING INFORMATION

Good information contributes to good decisions. Many communities recognize that a lack of quality information impedes the consideration of the full range of choices available to address the challenges they face. The federal government has data, information, and analytical tools that can be useful to communities. The role of the federal government is not to intrude in local decision-making. Rather, it is to provide America's communities with the capacity, knowledge, skills, information, and tools needed to make better local decisions. The information that decision-makers and communities seek includes technical data as well as information about policies, practices, and programs. The following initiatives will enhance local decision-making capacity.

Community/Federal Information Partnership

ISSUE: Communities across the nation are calling for greater assistance in addressing critical issues that affect their economic, social, and environmental wellbeing. America's communities need geographically-referenced data to make informed decisions that will ensure sustainable economic growth and a high quality of life. Communities are finding that this information has tremendous value in protecting the environment, fighting crime, advancing the public welfare, improving governmental efficiency, and safeguarding against natural disasters. Supporting this critical area of innovation will require improved integration and wider access to needed information through the development of a National Spatial Data Infrastructure. The Community/Federal Information Partnership (C/FIP) is designed to accelerate that development at the federal, state, tribal, and local levels.

ACTION: C/FIP BUDGET PROPOSAL

In their FY 2001 Budget proposals, the Department of Interior's U.S. Geological Survey (USGS) and the Department of Agriculture's Natural Resources Conservation Service (NRCS) have requested $35 million to support and expand the Community/Federal Information Partnership. These funds will support partnerships and projects across the country to develop local solutions to issues of both local and national concern, using biologic, geologic, hydrologic, soils, land cover, base maps, and other data from federal, state, and local sources. These investments in critical data infrastructure will help communities make more informed decisions. Of the total amount requested for FY 2001, approximately three-fourths will be allocated to competitively awarded matching grants and other cooperative agreements with communities. The remaining funds will help federal agencies make their geographic data more readily available to communities. Together these components will increase the capacity of communities to apply geographic data and tools to address the critical concerns facing their citizens, while promoting the full and rapid development of a National Spatial Data Infrastructure (NSDI).

ACTION: GEOSPATIAL INFORMATION DEMONSTRATION PROJECTS
The Federal Geographic Data Committee and the National Partnership for Reinventing Government have worked with federal agencies and local communities to develop six community demonstration projects to ensure that federal, state, and local information can be integrated and used for improved decision making at all levels of government. The NSDI Community Demonstration Projects give people access to geospatial information to make communities safer, environmentally cleaner, and more disaster-resistant. Policy lessons and accomplishments of these partnership projects will be released this year.

Livable America Indicators

ISSUE: The well-being of a community can be measured in many ways. Indicators of economic, social, and environmental health can be useful tools to help communities set priorities. Indicators highlight the issues and opportunities in communities and are necessary to track progress. When citizens, businesses, and local government come together and choose what is most important to measure with indicators, issues can be depolarized and relationships established to help a community reach consensus on ways to meet local challenges.

ACTION: The Federal Interagency Sustainable Development Indicators Group and the USDA Roundtable on Sustainable Forests will work with federal agencies, interested communities, and others to identify and compile a list of sample community-level indicators from which communities might choose to measure their progress toward becoming more livable. These indicators, as well as successful case studies of their use, will be made available on the National Livability Resource Center website <www.livablecommunities.gov>. The interagency group will also provide assistance to Community Partnerships (see pages 62-66) to incorporate livability indicators.

Community Livability Guides

ISSUE: Communities can benefit from better access to information about innovative strategies to address a range of livability issues. Community livability guides will produce information and best practices to tackle specific local challenges.

ACTION: The White House Task Force on Livable Communities is working with federal agencies to produce a series of guides to address the most pressing livability issues facing communities. The first guide, "Schools as Centers of Community: A Citizens' Guide for Planning and Design," was published by the Department of Education in May 2000. Possible subjects for additional guides include brownfields redevelopment; transit-oriented development; green infrastructure; energy efficiency and renewable energy; coastal growth; and linking hazard mitigation and livability. Easy access to these guides will be provided through the National Livability Resource Center website <www.livablecommunities.gov>.

Community Livability Toolbox

ISSUE: No matter how good or available information and data may be, its use is limited without the tools to properly understand and evaluate it. Design, visualization, impact analysis, and consensus-building tools have enormous potential for improving local decision-making. They help in the planning and design of sustainable and healthy communities by allowing planners and decision-makers to:

- Visualize design options;
- Increase integration of unique local and regional considerations;
- Involve a larger number of stakeholders in the planning process;
- Improve the quality of input from meeting participants;
- Assess development impacts and costs; and
- Improve modeling techniques and tools.

Decision support tools assist communities in making informed decisions by helping them understand the implications of different choices. Thus, these tools increase public involvement and help all participants make choices based on sound technical information. Unfortunately, many communities are either unaware of the array of tools available to them or they need assistance in determining which tools may be the most useful in addressing their needs.

ACTION: As the federal government develops tools for understanding, analyzing, and visualizing the vast array of existing information, it will ensure that the tools it has and develops are more useful and available to communities. Federal agencies will work to develop their tools collaboratively with state and local agencies and other organizations to ensure that federal tools are compatible with those used by communities. Specifically, federal agencies will undertake the following actions:

- **Identifying and Making Existing Tools Available.** Led by the Departments of Energy (DOE), Interior (DOI), and Transportation (DOT), the Environmental Protection Agency (EPA), and the U.S. Army Corps of Engineers (USACE), agencies will collaboratively identify a suite of information, visual and computer-based-analysis tools that may be useful to communities. The toolbox will be comprised of software tools such as Geographic Information System (GIS) programs, predictive models, impact analysis programs, and visualization programs. It will also include non-technical tools and resources, such as community visioning programs, interactive internet-based community networks, information resources, and group consensus building tools. Participating agencies will provide information on system requirements, data needs, start-up costs, compatibility with other tools, appropriate users of the tools, intended practical applications, and case studies describing how these tools are used. Information about identified and catalogued tools will be made available in a Community Livability Toolbox on the National Livability Resource Center website <www.livablecommunities.gov>.
- **Developing New Tools.** The Federal Geographic Data Committee, a federal interagency working group, will actively encourage greater communication and cooperation among federal agencies and between the federal government, communities, and

the private sector in the development of new decision-support tools. Several tools currently under development will soon be available to provide decision-support to communities as they address their livability concerns. Some of these new tools include:

- *The Smart Growth INDEX.* The EPA has developed the Smart Growth INDEX, a GIS-based planning tool for evaluating alternative growth, land use, and transportation scenarios for communities and regions. EPA will complete beta testing of the Smart Growth INDEX soon and make it available to some interested communities.

- *TRANSIMS: Transportation Analysis and Simulation System.* TRANSIMS is an advanced urban transportation/air quality analysis and forecasting model designed for local planning agencies to simulate the movement of vehicles and people for an entire metro region. It will permit the evaluation of a wider range of transportation options and allow decision-makers to make more informed choices to improve livability. DOT, in conjunction with DOE and EPA, will request community participation this summer for early deployment of TRANSIMS in a limited number of urban areas to test conversion from existing transportation forecasting models.

- *Natural Resources Planning Data.* The Department of Interior's U.S. Geological Survey (USGS) maintains a long-term collection of natural science and map data that can be very useful for community decision-making. This data and information should be part of the National Spatial Data Infrastructure, and be made available to citizens, communities and others. The USGS requested $2 million in FY 2001 to provide the infrastructure needed to more efficiently disseminate this type of scientific information to communities and decision-makers. This initiative will allow the agency to increase data transfer capacity, and improve the reliability and speed for data delivery, web pages, and real time data to communities.

- *Mapping Federal Investments in Land Conservation Programs.* The federal government operates numerous conservation programs across departmental and agency lines. The Department of Interior (DOI) will coordinate an interagency effort to collect and map all existing federal investments in land conservation into a single GIS database. The effort will include existing databases, such as the National Cooperative Soil Survey, National Resources Inventory, and the National Cooperative Geologic Mapping Program; federally owned lands; and locations of land enrolled in programs such as the Wetlands Reserve, Conservation Reserve, and Partners for Wildlife. The database will show the geographic distribution of federal conservation efforts and enable federal agencies, private land trusts, and state and local decision-makers to target assistance and resources to areas that need it most.

- *Data for Decision-Making.* DOT is funding a project under the National Academy of Sciences to work with local, state, and federal decision-makers involved in transportation, economic development, and land use planning activities to identify data needs for place-based decision-making. The project will identify the data and measures needed to make complex public decisions on transportation, land use planning, and economic development; identify opportunities to meet data needs and improve decision-support systems; and review plans of federal agencies to make needed data available to the public.

- ***Data for Economic Development Decision-Making.*** Sound technical information to address local economic development needs is essential to building and sustaining livable communities. The Department of Commerce's Economic Development Administration (EDA) is funding a web site <www.EconData.net> that provides state and local decision-makers easy access to the best economic data. The site includes more than 400 links to socioeconomic data sources, arranged by subject and provider, to facilitate finding and using regional economic data. A companion User's Guide (Socioeconomic Data for Understanding Your Regional Economy) is available on this site and on EDA's web site <www.doc.gov/eda>. The guide provides a comprehensive, easy-to-use reference for both novices and experienced data users to find and use economic statistics.
- ***HAZUS: Hazard Risk Assessment.*** Without a clear understanding of the risks associated with various natural hazards, it is difficult for many communities to introduce appropriate measures to protect the community. Communities may inadvertently promote growth in dangerous areas or allow building standards that do not offer adequate protection. The Federal Emergency Management Agency is developing a risk assessment tool, HAZUS, to assist states and local communities analyze and plan their actions to support more sustainable development. With the earthquake component already completed, this tool will soon incorporate modeling capabilities on flooding, both coastal and riverine, and wind, thereby enabling a fully multi-hazard approach to planning.

Community Livability Training

ISSUE: To better use information to reach their livability objectives, community leaders need to know what is available and how to use it. Training of this nature will help them make more informed decisions, better use available tools and information, learn about innovative strategies used in other communities, and work with developers to create new tools in needed areas. Federal employees also need training in a wide range of livable communities issues, including building collaborative partnerships with other federal agencies, with communities, and with regions.

ACTION: SMART GROWTH TRAINING

There is expanded interest in livability and smart growth among elected officials at all levels of government. This interest has created a demand for information and technical assistance as communities strive to achieve smarter growth. Opportunities to encourage smart growth exist at all levels of government, but coordination is essential to success. Development patterns are affected by local development policies, state land use laws and economic development incentives, and even a variety of federal policies. These factors all influence development.

Training is an essential prerequisite to intergovernmental coordination. Both governmental and non-governmental participants in the development process can more effectively work together to encourage smart growth when they are educated about the range of existing funding, regulatory, and non-regulatory programs at each level of government. The University of Maryland's School of Public Affairs developed a smart growth training course for state and local government officials and is currently planning a training course to integrate federal programs into the smart growth concept. Federal agencies whose areas of responsibility are key to smart growth, particularly in housing, rural and community development, transportation, and environmental and public health protection, will participate in and assist this intergovernmental training initiative. In addition, state, local, and non-governmental officials will participate in the development of course content.

ACTION: GREEN INFRASTRUCTURE TRAINING

Green infrastructure is our nation's natural life support system. It refers to the interconnected network of watersheds, woodlands, wildlife habitats, greenways, parks, working farms, ranches, forests, urban trees, parkways, and other connected open spaces that sustain and ensure quality of life when incorporated into local and regional plans, policies, and practices. These planned networks of open space link urban settings to rural ones and, like other infrastructure, become part of government operating budgets and management programs. Through training and subsequent local and regional planning and implementation activities, communities of all scales can benefit from the ecological, environmental, economic, and social contributions of green infrastructure.

The Department of Agriculture's U.S. Forest Service is facilitating an effort with other federal, state, and local government and non-profit partners to develop a training program to help communities make green infrastructure an inseparable part of local planning and decision making. Training would include conventional classroom courses, workshops, and forums, as well as hands-on, practical experiences. Activities include developing a "Green Infrastructure Resource Guide;" designing, piloting, and delivering an introductory green infrastructure course for state and local officials, non-profits, the private sector, and federal workers; documenting case studies; and disseminating green infrastructure information through conferences, forums, print media, and other opportunities.

ACTION: TRANSIT-ORIENTED DEVELOPMENT TRAINING

Creating livable communities requires real estate development that supports public transit and walking trips. Transit oriented development (TOD) and joint development use land in and around rail stations or bus transfer facilities. They offer a unique opportunity to create more livable places. TODs enhance livability by creating places that encourage transportation choice, reduce public service costs, co-locate community services, and increase housing affordability. Joint development of transit stations is important because it fosters partnerships among public transit systems and the private sector that can ensure long-term cash flow for transit agencies. Unfortunately, joint development has been limited by relatively little collaboration between public agencies and private developers in the past.

The Department of Transportation and the Environmental Protection Agency will establish training sessions for representatives from the real estate sector, transit agencies, communities, and federal agencies to learn about the benefits of TOD and joint development and to encourage interaction among stakeholders. To increase visibility and demonstrate commitment to community empowerment and growth as a tool for livability, sessions will be organized around local problem solving. For example, training sessions might consist of workshops in which stakeholders (finance, transit, community, and political leaders) meet to design TODs along existing or proposed transit stops using proven tools with experts in this area.

ACTION: HISTORIC PRESERVATION AND URBAN LOCATION TRAINING

The decisions that the federal government makes regarding caring for the nation's historic treasures and locating federal facilities are vital to communities across America. In partnership with the National Trust for Historic Preservation and local real estate developers, the General Services Administration (GSA) will provide executive and staff training across the country on how to accomplish historic preservation and urban location goals. In each session, GSA will present an overview of GSA's historic preservation and urban location programs, and share best practices and solutions to the challenges of accomplishing these goals within a customer-focused mission. The overview will be followed by an interactive roundtable discussion – with staff from the National Trust for Historic Preservation, GSA, a local developer, and representatives of other federal agencies – on solutions to specific obstacles GSA faces in striving to locate federal agencies in historic buildings and historic districts. Additional training will include a variety of preservation issues.

ACTION: TRANSPORTATION DESIGN TRAINING

The Department of Transportation will develop training modules and workshops for pedestrian and bicycle facility design.

- **Pedestrian Facility Design Course.** The design of facilities for pedestrians is a rapidly evolving field and a design guide for these facilities is currently being developed. The concept of "universal design" in which facilities are planned and designed to meet the needs of all users – including children, people with disabilities, and older persons – is an integral part of this course. The course is intended for planners, engineers, architects, and designers of other facilities for pedestrians, such as sidewalks and pathways.

- **Bicycle Facility Design Course.** This training course will build upon the information provided in "A Guide for the Development of Bicycle Facilities," recently published by the American Association of State Highway and Transportation Officials. The guide features designs of on and off road facilities for bicyclists. The intended audiences are planners and designers who provide facilities for bicyclists.

ACTION: COASTAL COMMUNITY TRAINING SERVICES

The National Oceanic and Atmospheric Administration's Coastal Services Center in Charleston, South Carolina, offers a range of training services to local coastal communities, including training at various levels in Geographic Information Systems. Training is also provided in coping with natural disasters, focusing on risk and vulnerability assessment, and community leadership and collaborative process skills.

ACTION: RURAL CAPACITY BUILDING

Rural communities often lack the capacity to bring residents together and engage in strategic planning that maps out a vision for future growth. USDA's Rural Community Assistance and Champion Community programs provide training, technical assistance, and funding to help rural communities prepare strategic plans. USDA also is helping rural nonprofit organizations develop the capacity to undertake economic development activities through its Rural Community Development Initiative. In addition, USDA's Cooperative Extension Network provides rural leaders and potential entrepreneurs training on entrepreneurial development strategies and the use of federal resources.

Community P.L.A.N.S. Teams

(Partnerships for Livability Among Neighborhoods and Schools)

ISSUE: Over the next ten years, thousands of schools will need to be built, and even more will need to be modernized, to respond to rising enrollments and to repair aging schools. In many communities, the need for reinvestment in the nation's public school facilities is viewed as an opportunity to explore ways that schools can become safer and healthier places for children to learn; more efficient facilities to operate; and serve as centers of the community. Rather than creating facilities that are only open from 9 to 3, communities are considering how schools can be centers of learning and recreation for the entire community. It is crucial that administrators, parents, teachers, and community members involved in the planning and design of these new schools and renovation projects have access to the best information concerning the choices available to them. These choices will not only enhance the educational experience for children, but will also strengthen the integral relationships between schools and the larger community, including businesses, public, civic, and private organizations.

ACTION: The Department of Education will lead an interagency team to identify federal resources to help communities in the design of new schools and the modernization of existing ones. The interagency team – including the Environmental Protection Agency (EPA), Federal Emergency Management Agency (FEMA), U.S. Army Corps of Engineers (USACE), and the Departments of Energy (DOE), Justice (DOJ), Interior (DOI), and Agriculture (USDA) – will identify how federal resources can support community livability goals in the school design process. The Department of Education will serve as a clearinghouse to package technical assistance resources to assist school districts in building and renovating schools. Federal resources include:

- **Schools as Centers of Community**. The Department of Education will gather and disseminate best practices for designing schools as centers of communities;
- **Location Decisions.** EPA can help communities understand the impact of school location decisions on future growth patterns in the community;
- **Energy Efficiency**. DOE can help school districts identify ways to reduce energy bills and enhance educational productivity by utilizing natural light;
- **Public Safety**. DOJ has a number of funding and technical assistance programs available to help design schools with basic safety principles;
- **Indoor Air Quality.** EPA can provide technical assistance to help schools create a healthy indoor environment for children;
- **Disaster Resistance.** FEMA can help school officials plan for disaster, decrease risk, protect the safety of students and educators, and ensure that schools recover quickly;
- **Open Space.** USDA and DOI can provide funding and technical assistance to design and build outdoor learning centers and parks; plant trees; and develop educational resources; and
- **Contracting Assistance.** The Army Corps of Engineers can assist school districts in scoping, negotiating, awarding, administering, and terminating contracts.

Guidance for Using Water and Wastewater Funding

ISSUE: Water and sewer systems are necessary for growth, but it is estimated that sprawl can inflate water and sewer infrastructure costs by 20 to 40 percent. State revolving funds give states and localities a powerful tool to influence growth patterns and save tens of billions of taxpayer dollars over the long run.

ACTION: The Environmental Protection Agency and its state and local partners are developing guidance on how to operate Wastewater and Drinking Water State Revolving Funds to promote smart growth. Many states, such as Maryland, use water and sewer policies to promote smart growth. This guidance will share "lessons-learned" and provide specific program options for promoting smart growth.

Some examples include offering points in the state's priority ranking system for projects that encompass smart growth principles; providing loans for land acquisition or purchase of development rights on protected land; and using loans to remediate brownfields sites. Some states could even require municipalities to adopt zoning or long-term comprehensive growth plans in order to receive Clean Water State Revolving Funds. Not all types of projects may be practical or even possible in all states, but the booklet will be a starting point for states to learn from each other on ways to support smart growth with the state revolving funds.

Livable Community Resource Centers

ISSUE: Many state and federal programs intended to resolve specific community problems often fail to achieve their objectives because communities lack the capacity to respond. Communities may be unaware of programs, unable to fulfill the program application requirements, or unable to implement programs effectively to meet their particular local needs. The growing devolution of federal and state programs to the local level adds to the burden of finding sustainable local solutions. Furthermore, many smaller communities have very limited capacity to respond to needs because they lack a critical mass of resources and skills. Resource centers can address these needs by providing access to resources and skills.

In particular, the learning curve involved in using computer and audio-visual tools to analyze local development can be significantly accelerated if the federal government assists tool makers and users to share information and lessons learned. Resource centers create real or virtual places, where tool users can exchange information, learn about new tools and data, and query government officials on how best to access and use national and regional data bases.

ACTION: THE NATIONAL LIVABILITY RESOURCE CENTER

A team of federal agencies, including the Environmental Protection Agency, General Services Administration, U.S. Army Corps of Engineers, and the Departments of Commerce, Energy, Interior, Transportation, and Housing and Urban Development will develop an internet-based National Livability Resource Center to serve as a clearinghouse for decision-support data, information, tools, and federal programs and resources. The Center, to be located at <www.livablecommunities.gov>, will feature the following:

- A reference guide to federal data that regions and communities may need for local analysis;
- A mechanism to query appropriate federal officials on how to access critical data;
- Information on practices that address specific livability concerns, including community guides;
- A catalog of, and links to, federal resources and programs that support livability decisions;
- An inventory of effective decision-support software, hardware, and audio-visual resources;
- Technical assistance services; and
- A mechanism to allow communities and federal agencies to share best practices and experiences with one another.

Sponsoring federal agencies will work with organizations familiar with conducting comprehensive community assessments to identify data and tools critical for community decision-support. The National Livability Resource Center will reference this data, create links where the data is available on the Internet and provide contact information where web links are not available.

ACTION: REGIONAL RESOURCE CENTERS

Many local issues affecting livability are regional in nature. Consequently, solutions to growth problems often require regional collaboration. Localities can benefit from regional collaboration on acquiring and accessing decision-support tools. Good data and state-of-the-art computer tools can be costly, both to acquire and to maintain, but regional sharing of these investments can make decision-support tools more affordable. In addition, operating these tools at the regional level will help ensure that localities within the region are evaluating their development with a common foundation of information and assumptions, making regional impact assessments and joint decisions easier.

Several communities around the country have begun efforts to establish Regional Resource Centers (RRCs), or Urban Design Centers, equipped with decision-support tools to better deal with land use, resource use, and quality of life issues on a regional scale. The Departments of Agriculture, Energy, Interior, and Commerce, the Environmental Protection Agency, and other interested agencies will work with these communities to help make RRCs a success. Pilot RRCs will be created in both urban and rural areas such as those areas served by Metropolitan Planning Organizations, Councils of Government, or Regional Planning Commissions. The USDA's four Regional Rural Development Centers will also play a lead role in the establishment of Rural RRCs. Each RRC will be open to all local stakeholders – including elected officials, zoning administrators, land-use planners, real estate developers, and neighborhood and environmental organizations. In particular, the RRCs will provide information, modeling, applied research and other assistance to help stakeholders evaluate and understand the short- and long-term consequences of their development decisions on the economy, environment, and social fabric of the region. Pilot RRCs will be encouraged to use a consortium of local organizations and universities to provide technical expertise for analysis.

BEING A GOOD NEIGHBOR

The federal government manages buildings, lands, and its workforce in communities across the country. In these communities, the federal government has an obligation to be a good neighbor and ensure that its actions support – not hinder – community efforts to achieve livability goals. From working closely with communities to catalyze smart development, to helping communities adapt to military base closings, to encouraging federal workers to use alternative transportation, this section details several initiatives designed to make the federal sector a better neighbor in America's communities.

Managing Federal Assets to Promote Livability

ISSUE: The federal government is the largest employer and manager of physical assets in the country. The federal presence significantly affects community quality of life. Being a good neighbor in local communities requires the federal government to manage these assets in a manner that is mindful and supportive of local goals.

ACTION: GOOD NEIGHBOR PRINCIPLES

The General Services Administration's (GSA) work in communities will be guided by the following seven Good Neighbor Principles:

1. Make strategic, regional, location decisions.
   - Strategic real estate planning with central cities and inner suburbs.
   - Implement Executive Orders 12072 and 13006 directing federal agencies to locate in downtowns and historic buildings and districts.
2. Promote community involvement and partnerships.
   - Ensure full participation from local partners.
3. Offer transportation alternatives.
   - Examples include helping to create walkable neighborhoods and development near transit.
4. Invest in infill and urban locations.
   - Examples include locating in central business and historic districts, reusing historic buildings, and participating in downtown management organizations.
5. Seek ways to leverage investment.
   - Examples include forming partnerships with communities, other agencies and private businesses.
6. Promote mixed-use, live-work-play, 24-hour cities.
   - Examples include "outleasing" historic buildings to private property owners, leasing in mixed-use buildings, and providing restaurants and shops in ground floors of federal buildings.
7. Consider the effect of technology on space needs.
   - Examples include providing live-work alternatives.

ACTION: LEASING FEDERAL PROPERTY

GSA proposes to amend the Federal Property and Administrative Services Act of 1949 to enable, among other things, federal agencies to lease underutilized real property to private parties for development or redevelopment. These public-private partnerships would allow federal real property to better support community development. These partnerships would be structured so they do not violate federal budget scoring rules, which are different from the accounting rules used in state and local partnerships with private developers.

Transportation Alternatives for Federal Employees

ISSUE: There are over two million federal civilian (defense and non-defense) employees. The federal government can set an example for all public and private sector employers by promoting alternatives to single occupancy vehicle commuting for its employees.

ACTION: IMPLEMENT EXECUTIVE ORDER

In order to reduce federal employees' contribution to traffic congestion and air pollution and to expand their commuting alternatives, President Clinton signed an executive order on April 21, 2000 that includes three major provisions:

- **Federal Agencies in the National Capital Region.** By October 1, 2000, federal agencies in the National Capital Region will offer their employees up to $65 per month ($100, beginning in 2002) in "transit pass" benefits to commute to work by transit or eligible vanpools. The agency can pay for the benefit using existing appropriated funds, usually taken from administrative accounts such as salaries, benefits, and travel. Employees will receive the benefit completely free of all payroll taxes, federal income taxes, and Virginia, D.C., and Maryland state income taxes.

- **Federal Agencies Nationwide.** By October 1, 2000, federal agencies, outside of the National Capital Region, will permit their employees to use pre-tax income to pay transit or eligible vanpool costs of up to a maximum of $65 per month ($100, beginning in 2002). Employees save on federal payroll and income taxes on the amount of the benefit they purchase, since that amount is no longer treated or reported as taxable salary. Agencies' payroll costs are reduced since payroll taxes do not apply to the funds used for the benefit.

- **Nationwide 3-Year Pilot Program.** By October 1, 2000, the Departments of Transportation and Energy, and the Environmental Protection Agency will offer their employees nationwide up to $65 per month ($100, beginning in 2002) in "transit pass" benefits to commute to work by transit or eligible vanpools. Before determining if this program should be extended to federal employees nationwide, it will be analyzed to determine its effectiveness in reducing single occupancy vehicle travel and local area congestion.

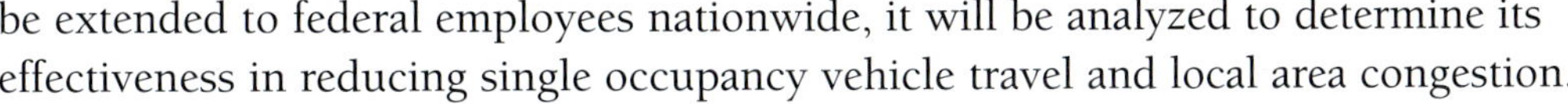

ACTION: GSA'S TRANSPORTATION CHOICES INITIATIVE

The General Services Administration is committed to offering and promoting real choices to federal commuters and visitors in travelling to and from federal buildings. The agency will explore:

- Creating an initiative to install a bike rack in every federal building;
- Promoting existing facilities in buildings such as showers and lockers;
- Installing kiosks in federal buildings to dispense mass transit tickets to federal employees and visitors; and
- Ensuring that new federal buildings are mass transit, bicycle, and pedestrian-friendly.

Livability in Redevelopment of Former Military Bases

ISSUE: Military base closures seriously affect surrounding communities that must transition away from an economy that developed to serve the base. As communities redevelop, they face many options as they seek to turn a liability into a community asset. For those that wish to redevelop with livability principles, the federal government can help.

ACTION: The Department of Defense (DOD) will provide Local Redevelopment Authorities (LRAs) at Base Realignment and Closures (BRAC) sites with a multi-agency package of technical assistance to help impacted communities including those communities that wish to redevelop using the principles of livability. The LRAs are composed of respected and responsible community leaders, and DOD provides financial support for their work. Many former BRAC sites have experienced remarkable success in redevelopment and community revitalization. Even greater opportunities for economic development exist now that the FY 2000 Defense Authorization Act allows DOD to transfer BRAC sites at no cost to LRAs for economic development and job creation. No-cost transfers, combined with special livability resources, will continue to enhance community revitalization efforts.

Growth in Communities Surrounded by Federal Lands

ISSUE: In many communities in the West, development cannot occur in a meaningful, coordinated manner without considering the use of public lands. To address this need, the Department of Interior's Bureau of Land Management (BLM) has identified certain lands as potentially available for sale or disposal to allow communities to expand and economically develop in ways that make sense for them. Nonetheless, land development often carries attendant problems of increasing concern to local communities, including loss of land for recreation, species habitat, and other open space uses, such as farming and grazing. While some sales or exchanges proceed smoothly, the process can be time consuming and contentious as communities decide how and where growth should occur. Through land sale and disposal initiatives, BLM can assist local communities in planning for and facilitating the transfer of federal lands to promote both economic growth and high quality of life.

ACTION: BLM is seeking additional land disposal tools similar to those available under the Southern Nevada Land Management Act, which streamlined the procedures for sale or exchange of certain federally owned, BLM-managed lands within a limited area of the Las Vegas valley. The Act made it possible for BLM to transfer land to the community to accommodate the city's growth, and allowed BLM to use proceeds from such transfers to purchase and protect environmentally sensitive land elsewhere in the State of Nevada. BLM supports proposed legislation that would provide similar authority for BLM in other jurisdictions. This legislation would enable BLM to work with local jurisdictions and private interests to facilitate the transfer of some federal lands identified in land use plans as potentially available for disposal while ensuring that open space is preserved. Areas covered would include recreational areas, riparian and wildlife habitat, and significant historical, archaeological, and cultural sites.

Managing the Wildland/Urban Interface

ISSUE: The last decade has seen unprecedented growth in many cities and towns in the West. This growth, which is projected to continue, changes both the way communities relate to surrounding public lands and their expectations. The federal government oversees significant acreage both within and near rapidly growing urban and rural communities. These areas, known as the "wildland/urban interface," have become the focus of interest for city and county governments, land developers, and the environmental community. Changing values about public land management and more and different demands for public land resources have exacerbated environmental concerns such as maintaining healthy air standards, preventing water source depletion, preventing forests fires, maintaining water quality, and preventing fragmentation of critical wildlife habitat. As growth in the wildland/urban interface continues, issues such as development patterns, the need for transportation and utility corridors, the demand for increasing and varied recreational uses, public safety, and preserving open space will all contribute to heightened interest in, and conflicts on, these lands.

ACTION: BLM LAND USE PLANNING

The President's FY 2001 Budget request includes $19 million for the Interior Department's Bureau of Land Management (BLM) to update land use planning. Most of BLM's 162 land use plans are at least 10 to 15 years old and do not meet the requirements of the National Environmental Policy Act. These aging plans must be updated to address areas with vulnerable, sensitive, or at risk resource values. Land use plans are the basis for every action the BLM takes and serve as its primary tool for building consensus and providing the public a voice in BLM's land and resource management programs. The BLM plan updates would also be adaptable to changing conditions and demands of the growing West.

ACTION: FIREWISE PREVENTION PROGRAM

The Forest Service, the Department of the Interior, the National Association of State Foresters, and the National Fire Protection Association have launched Firewise, a new initiative working with state, local, and private partners to promote wildland fire safety. The Firewise initiative promotes community projects through adult education, community action planning, fuel treatments, and landscaping. In 2000 and 2001, nine regional workshops are scheduled throughout the United States to encourage local policy makers, insurance executives, real estate executives, bankers, and community planners to establish local planning, landscaping, and building standards to assure a safer place for people to live. For more information, visit <www.firewise.org>.

Promoting Livability in Gateway Communities

ISSUE: Communities that serve as the entry points into adjacent public recreational lands are often called "gateway" communities. These communities and the national parks and other public recreational lands that border them are inextricably linked by local economies, cultural identity, and quality of life. Because these public lands often draw large numbers of recreational visitors, gateway communities can experience sudden and extreme development pressures. They may face serious growth management problems with transportation, increases in living costs, and the proliferation of tourist-oriented businesses, resulting in direct impacts on community livability and the recreational experience of visitors. This interdependence provides an opportunity for public land managers and gateway communities to work together to address area-wide transportation planning, economic development, and land-use issues.

ACTION: To assist gateway communities with addressing some of these problems more effectively, the Department of the Interior (DOI), in cooperation with other federal agencies and non-profits, has developed a Gateway Community Initiative. The initiative provides the following:

- The National Park Service (NPS) has prepared a Transportation Planning Guidebook for gateway communities and national park and federal land managers. The guide offers technical assistance, best practices, and success stories on partnering with gateway communities and state, regional, and local governments to coordinate transportation planning efforts.
- The NPS, with support from the Department of Transportation, developed an online resource center to provide information to communities and public land managers on transportation planning initiatives, including the Transportation Equity Act for the 21st Century, alternative transportation projects, training, personnel exchange opportunities, and frequently asked questions.
- Building on existing efforts, the DOI, other federal land management agencies, the Sonoran Institute, and The Conservation Fund will partner to offer regional and local training courses for public land managers and community leaders. The courses will cover planning for and balancing the demands and pressures of recreation and commerce in communities adjacent to public lands.

BUILDING PARTNERSHIPS

Collaboration works. The growing national livable communities movement offers exciting opportunities for new partnerships. These partnerships cross many of the traditional boundaries that have kept people apart. Partnerships are emerging across issues, as people realize that livable communities policies and practices can foster economic prosperity, environmental quality, and a higher quality of life for all Americans. Partnerships are emerging across sectors, as business, state and local governments, farmers, urban activists, and environmentalists realize the common ground they share. And partnerships are emerging across the American landscape as cities, suburbs, and rural areas recognize that regional approaches to problem solving can produce benefits for everyone.

To be effective, the Livable Communities Initiative must include opportunities for the federal government to work directly in partnership with communities where Americans live, work, play, and learn. To do this, the Administration has entered into a variety of collaborative partnerships with communities, regions, the private sector, non-profits, and academic institutions in places across the country. These partnerships are test beds for innovative approaches to building livable communities, and the lessons learned will be broadly applied in America's communities in the future.

The Partnership for Regional Livability

The Partnership for Regional Livability (PRL) is not a typical federal program. In fact, it's not a federal program at all. It's a true partnership that emerged from discussions that began in 1998 among several major national foundations and an informal team representing the executive branch of the federal government. With time, it has become an effort to help civic leaders in regions across America address large-scale, intractable problems. Drawing on a national network of experts, PRL (or, 'Pearl') delivers technical assistance to regions. It organizes a region's access to federal government expertise and resources, with the cooperation of local and state elected officials. It helps develop federal readiness and capacity to work with regions. And it helps regions build supportive relationships with each other, exchange information, and share tools and lessons learned.

The Partnership's pilot regions include the metropolitan areas surrounding Atlanta, Chicago, Denver, and the San Francisco Bay. The five initial projects address some of the most difficult challenges facing our country: cleaning up air pollution; connecting poor, inner-city job seekers to jobs sprouting in suburbs; preventing sprawl into the countryside and congestion on the roadways; attracting private investment for housing and businesses in impoverished neighborhoods; and protecting the quality of drinking water. The projects all promote livable communities and have the potential to significantly improve the quality of life in the target regions.

One of the primary goals of PRL is to identify a new role for the federal government in support of regional initiatives. Instead of putting the burden on the regions to figure out how to make sense of a wide variety of federal programs and resources, PRL turns that the conventional approach on its head. This new way of working with the federal government is based on the concept of a "Reverse RFP." Rather than navigating the federal maze on its own, the region will determine its own priorities and issue a "Reverse RFP – or Request for Partnership" – to the federal government.

The burden is then placed on the federal government to determine how its resources can be aligned to support the region's goals. The RFP does not necessarily mean new financial resources for a region. But it will mean much easier access to existing federal resources coordinated across agency boundaries. From the federal standpoint, this innovative approach provides federal agencies a creative way to work in partnership with regions and other federal agencies to fulfill their core missions.

PRL projects are in various stages of development, with more than a dozen federal agencies participating in discussions about how the federal government can add value to the regional projects using existing authorities. The following summaries describe PRL projects that are currently underway:

Atlanta, Georgia: The Chattahoochee Riverway Project

Description: The purpose of the Chattahoochee Riverway Project is to implement a bold vision for urban, suburban, and rural growth in northwest Georgia within the Chattahoochee River watershed. The project will develop and implement a coordinated watershed management and protection strategy that will support the protection of an average of 500 feet of buffer lands along 215 miles of the river. The project will include monitoring and enhancing water quality in the river and its tributaries, a source of drinking water for more than half of all Georgians, and establishing a regional park system. The Chattahoochee Riverway Project is part of a broader regional and state initiative to support livable communities and combat sprawl throughout northwest Georgia.

Local Supporters: Mayor Campbell and the City of Atlanta, Chattahoochee Nature Center, City of Columbus, City of Douglasville, City of Duluth, City of Franklin, City of Helen, City of Roswell, Carroll County, Coweta County, Douglas County, Forsyth County, Fulton County, Georgia

Chamber of Commerce, Georgia Conservancy, Gwinnett County, Hall County, Heard County, State of Georgia (including Governor Barnes and the State Department of Natural Resources), The Nature Conservancy, The Upper Chattahoochee Riverkeeper, Trust for Public Land, Turner Foundation, White County, and the Woodruff Foundation.

Federal Partners: Interior (lead agency), Agriculture (Forest Service & Natural Resources Conservation Service), U.S. Army Corps of Engineers, Army Environmental Policy Institute, Environmental Protection Agency, Federal Emergency Management Agency, and Transportation.

Chicago Metropolitan Region, Illinois: Clean Air Counts

Description: The Chicago metro region faces both public health and economic ramifications from non-compliance with the requirements of the Clean Air Act. The purpose of Clean Air Counts is to identify innovative strategies to bring the region into compliance with air quality standards in a manner that is consistent with economic development goals. PRL is adding value to this ongoing local initiative by bringing all appropriate federal agencies to the table.

Local Supporters: Chicago Mayor Daley and the Metropolitan Mayors Caucus, Governor Ryan and appropriate state agencies, the Delta Institute, the MacArthur Foundation, the Grand Victoria Foundation, and the local business community, labor, academics, and community-based organizations.

Federal Partners: Environmental Protection Agency (lead agency), Agriculture, Commerce (Economic Development Administration & National Oceanic and Atmospheric Administration), Energy, General Services Administration, Health and Human Services, Housing & Urban Development, Interior, and Transportation.

Denver Metropolitan Region, Colorado: Metro Denver Works

Description: *Metro Denver Works* is a proposed public-private partnership initially aimed to address spatial mismatch issues in metro Denver – on the regional, subregional, and individual jurisdiction scale. Using GIS mapping and land use modeling tools, *Metro Denver Works* focuses on the links between jobs, housing, childcare, and transportation and identifies strategies to alleviate conflicts among them. Overall, the goal is to improve the efficiency (economic and energy/resource) of metropolitan Denver. Key issues *Metro Denver Works* aims to answer include: a) location – how to locate housing projects near potential jobs and new businesses near concentrations of housing and potential employees; b) access – how can businesses and public agencies improve accessibility of jobs, childcare, training, and other critical services for people that could fill needed jobs; c) affordability – what strategies can businesses and public agencies pursue to make housing and transportation more affordable, supporting the long-term viability of employer/employee relationships; and d) smart growth – how can spatial alignment strategies better match the landscape with respect to environmental concerns, neighborhood livability, and promoting a sense of place for neighborhoods.

This work will serve as the foundation for a policy initiative – JOB NETwork – to increase the knowledge base and common understandings among policy makers of the importance of regional cooperation in workforce development; and a performance initiative – JOB SUPPORT – to determine the practical opportunities and challenges of building the capacity to act regionally.

Local Supporters: Mayor Webb and the City of Denver, Denver Metro Chamber of Commerce/Metro Denver Network (business), and the Denver Regional Council of Governments (government).

Federal Partners: Energy and Labor (lead agencies), Health and Human Services, Housing and Urban Development, and Transportation.

San Francisco Bay Region, California: The Community Capital Investment Initiative

Description: The purpose of the Community Capital Investment Initiative (CCII) is to create a mechanism to engage business, community, and government leadership in the use of market forces and access to capital to reduce poverty and create healthy and prosperous communities in the 46 communities in the Bay Area with concentrated persistent poverty. CCII will focus on identifying and encouraging completion of keystone mixed-use, mixed-income housing, commercial, industrial, and business developments that will create significant deal-flow and lead to economic, social, and environmental benefits in the targeted communities and among its residents.

Local Supporters: Bay Area Alliance for Sustainable Development – a multi-stakeholder coalition of 45 organizations composed of economic, environmental, and social equity as well as local government representation. Founding steering committee members of the Alliance are the Association of Bay Area Governments, Bay Area Council (business), PG&E, Sierra Club, and Urban Habitat (environmental justice). In addition, mayors from East Palo Alto, Oakland, Richmond, and San Francisco have expressed support for CCII.

Federal Partners: Housing and Urban Development (lead agency), Agriculture, Commerce (Economic Development Administration), Defense, Environmental Protection Agency, Federal Reserve, General Services Administration, Health and Human Services, Labor, Small Business Administration, Transportation, and Treasury.

San Francisco Bay Region, California: The Bay Area Livability Footprint

Description: The Bay Area Livability Footprint will depict a graphic geographic display of the land use implications of the principle 10 Commitments to Action contained in the *Draft Compact for A Sustainable Bay Area.* This geographic display will provide a crucial decision-making tool by mapping alternative future growth, natural resource preservation, and community revitalization scenarios with the aim of achieving consensus on where to grow and where not develop in the Bay Area. The purpose of the Footprint project is to use state-of-the-art information and planning tools to help communities throughout the Bay Area region identify and implement alternative development options that ultimately will reverse the current urban trends of inefficient land use, heavy traffic congestion, inner-city disinvestment, and ecological degradation.

Local Supporters: Bay Area Alliance for Sustainable Development – a multi-stakeholder coalition of 45 organizations composed of economic, environmental and social equity as well as local government representation. Founding steering committee members of the Alliance are the Association of Bay Area Governments, Bay Area Council (business), PG&E, Sierra Club, and Urban Habitat (environmental justice).

Federal Partners: Interior (lead agency), Commerce (National Oceanic and Atmospheric Administration), Environmental Protection Agency, Housing & Urban Development, and Transportation.

Community Partnerships

To gain additional on-the-ground experience with livable communities issues, the Clinton-Gore Administration has also launched a Community Partnerships initiative. Modeled on the Partnership for Regional Livability (PRL), the Community Partnership initiative focuses on an additional 11 pilot areas. The primary differences from PRL are that some of these partnerships will be at the neighborhood scale; some will be with mid-sized cities; and some will be in rural areas. But like PRL, these partnerships will demonstrate how the federal government can best align its resources to support locally determined livable communities' goals. These partnerships will reflect the diversity of communities and the issues facing them, but they will all be based on one fundamental principle: *communities know best*. The federal government will not substitute its judgment for that of the community; its role in the partnership is to play a supportive role by marshalling federal resources where they can be most helpful to the community.

Under the leadership of the White House Task Force on Livable Communities, Community Partnerships are underway in the following places:

Brownsville, Texas: Revitalizing Downtown

Description: The city is working to spur economic development as it revitalizes its downtown and protects its natural resources. Brownsville Mayor Vela is initiating a multifaceted program with projects involving downtown revitalization, economic development, eco-tourism, disaster prevention, natural resource conservation, and development of historic sites. This program includes substantial efforts from the HUD Community Builder program. All of these elements are key in plans to make Brownsville a more livable community and to celebrate the heritage of Rio Grande Communities. The plan is to collaborate throughout the process with all parties that have an interest in making Brownsville a better place to live and work.

Local Supporters: Mayor Vela and the City of Brownsville, Brownsville Community Foundation, Consortium of the Rio Grande (CoRio), Rio Grande Institute, Texas Historical Commission, and the University of Texas at Brownsville.

Federal Partners: General Services Administration (lead agency), U.S. Army Corps of Engineers, Commerce (Economic Development Administration & National Oceanic and Atmospheric Administration), Environmental Protection Agency, Executive Office of the President (Council on Environmental Quality), Federal Emergency Management Agency, Housing & Urban Development, Interior (Fish & Wildlife Service & National Park Service), International Boundary and Water Commission, and Transportation (Coast Guard).

Southeast Kentucky: Building a Prosperous Future

Description: Federal agencies are partnering with citizen-lead action teams to develop innovative approaches to solve long-standing problems. Highlights of the effort include strategies to overcome the digital divide; convening farmers to develop alternative agricultural markets; and identifying small business incubator opportunities.

Local Supporters: Mountain Association for Community Economic Development; Owsley and Breathitt Counties Action Teams.

Federal Partners: Agriculture (lead agency), Appalachian Regional Commission, Commerce (Economic Development Administration), Education, Energy, Environmental Protection Agency, Health & Human Services, Housing & Urban Development, Interior, Small Business Administration, and Transportation.

Eastern North Carolina: Recovering from Disaster

Description: Hurricane Floyd's devastating impact left many of North Carolina's eastern communities at a crossroads for reconstruction decisions. Communities in the 26 most affected counties are fighting to rebuild for a stronger future. Rather than simply replacing what was lost, these communities are seeking to rebuild in ways that make them more equitable, prosperous, and effective. The focus will be to build local capacity to develop sustainable and disaster-proof communities, economies, and environments (especially in planning, geographic information and mapping capacity); establish ongoing, collaborative, and mentoring relationships among communities; identify and implement inclusive, community-based redevelopment projects that promote recovery, sustainability, and collaboration; and identify policy issues that can facilitate livability in rural communities and disaster-affected areas.

Local Supporters: Governor Jim Hunt and the State of North Carolina, Center for Geographic Information and Analysis, North Carolina Rural Economic Development Center, The Conservation Fund, county and town officials, nonprofit organizations, and local business leaders.

Federal Partners: Federal Emergency Management Agency and the Commerce Department's Economic Development Administration (lead agencies), Agriculture, U.S. Army Corps of Engineers, Commerce (National Oceanic and Atmospheric Administration), Energy, Environmental Protection Agency, General Services Administration, Housing & Urban Development, Interior (Geological Survey), National Aeronautics and Space Administration, National Endowment for the Arts, National Partnership for Reinventing Government, Small Business Administration, and Transportation.

Hartford, Connecticut: Expanding Transportation Choices

Description: The project aims to coordinate and link existing transportation, land use, and economic development activities at both the neighborhood and regional level to increase transportation options and job opportunities for local residents, and to foster public/private investment in underinvested areas.

Local Supporters: Capital Region Council of Governments, Mayor Peters and the City of Hartford, Connecticut State Departments of Transportation, Labor, and Social Services, Parkville Area of West Hartford, and West Hartford.

Federal Partners: Transportation (lead agency – Federal Aviation Administration, Federal Highway Administration, Federal Railroad Administration, Federal Transit Administration, National Highway Traffic Safety Administration, & Office of Motor Carriers), Agriculture, Energy, Environmental Protection Agency, General Services Administration, Health & Human Services, Housing & Urban Development, Interior, Justice, and Postal Service.

Los Angeles, California: Making Schools the Centers of Communities

Description: This project will bring together community, state, and national leaders in education, architecture, business, community development, finance, environment, government, and local health to define and plan 21st century schools as community centers and develop strategies to implement them in Los Angeles.

Local Supporters: Advancement Project, Community Partners, Division of the State Architect, Getty Education Institute of the Arts, Los Angeles Unified School District, Metropolitan Forum Project, Proposition BB's Citizen Oversight Committee, and the Urban Land Institute's Los Angeles District Council.

Federal Partners: Education (lead agency), Agriculture, Energy, Environmental Protection Agency, Federal Emergency Management Agency, Health & Human Services, Housing & Urban Development, Interior, and Justice.

Omaha, Nebraska: Restoring the Riverfront

Description: This partnership will assist the City of Omaha to use the riverfront as a source of vitality for the city. The focus will be on redevelopment activities that are influenced by and will enhance the environment of the Missouri River. This will include brownfields cleanup and reuse, river-oriented interpretive and recreational facilities, natural resource restoration, and infrastructure rehabilitation.

Local Supporters: Mayor Daub and the City of Omaha, BRW Inc., City of Carter Lake, Iowa, Inner City Coalition on the Environment, States of Nebraska and Iowa, and Union Pacific Railroad.

Federal Partners: U.S. Army Corps of Engineers (lead agency), Environmental Protection Agency, Housing & Urban Development, Interior (National Park Service), Transportation (Coast Guard & Air Force).

Philadelphia, Pennsylvania: Institutional Investment in Urban Communities

Description: This partnership will strengthen and expand the University of Pennsylvania partnership with the City and the West Philadelphia neighborhoods surrounding the University of Pennsylvania campus and university district. Key elements include increasing public safety, rehabilitating housing, increasing home ownership, spurring economic development, and fostering excellent public schools.

Local Supporters: University of Pennsylvania, Mayor Street and the City of Philadelphia, Fannie Mae, West Philadelphia Partnership, School District of Philadelphia, Philadelphia Federation of Teachers, University City District, West Philadelphia Enterprise Center, and local businesses.

Federal Partners: Housing & Urban Development (lead agency), Agriculture, U.S. Army Corps of Engineers, Commerce (Economic Development Administration), Education, Energy, Environmental Protection Agency, Interior, Justice, National Endowment for the Arts, and Transportation.

Riverside County, California: Planning for Smart Growth

Description: Riverside County, among the largest and fastest-growing counties in the United States, is in the process of developing and implementing a comprehensive program, the Riverside County Integrated Project (RCIP) to address environmental, transportation, and land use needs well into the 21st Century. The process uses an inclusive approach that addresses both the legal requirements of state and federal law and incorporates the vision articulated by the County's residents. It includes three components: (1) multi-species habitat conservation, open space, and wetlands planning that will preserve open space, species habitat and recreation values for the County's residents; (2) transportation and communication corridor planning designed to relieve transportation bottlenecks while shaping sensible growth patterns for decades to come; and (3) updating the County's General Plan.

Local Supporters: Audubon Society, Building Industry Association, Chambers of Commerce, Coachella Valley Association of Governments, Endangered Habitats League, Friends of the North San Jacinto Valley, Hemet-San Jacinto Action Group, Monday Morning Group, Murrieta-Temecula Group, Riverside County Board Supervisors, Riverside County Farm Bureau, Riverside County Transportation Commission, Riverside Land Trust, Riverside Private Property Owners Association, Sierra Club, Southern California Association of Governments, State of California, The Nature Conservancy, The Valley Group, Tri-County Conservation League, Union for River Greenbelt Environment, and the Western Riverside Council of Governments.

Federal Partners: Interior (lead agency), Agriculture (Forest Service & Natural Resources Conservation Service), U.S. Army Corps of Engineers, Environmental Protection Agency, and Transportation.

Rochester, New York: Supporting Renaissance

Description: The City of Rochester will work with federal agencies to implement the City's comprehensive long-term plan, *Rochester 2010: The Renaissance Plan.* The partnership will focus on several specific projects designed to revitalize Rochester as the social, economic, and cultural core of the surrounding region as well as demonstrate the need for regional growth planning. Specifically, proposed projects involve revitalizing housing and economic development along the Genesee River; restoring the City's harbor into a social, cultural, and recreational destination point; and creating a GIS-based map and demonstration of regional growth planning in the greater Rochester area.

Local Supporters: Mayor Johnson and the City of Rochester, Common Good Planning Center, Genesee Fingerlakes Regional Planning Council, Rochester Area Community Foundation, and local faith-based organizations.

Federal Partners: Interior and Housing & Urban Development (lead agencies), Agriculture, U.S. Army Corps of Engineers, Commerce (Economic Development Administration), Education, Energy, Environmental Protection Agency, General Services Administration, Justice, National

Endowment for the Arts, Transportation (Federal Highway Administration & Federal Transit Administration).

San Diego, California: Green Energy for a Better Future

Description: This effort focuses on addressing the serious capacity shortfall of projected energy needs for the City of San Diego within the next few years by developing alternative fuel sources for transportation such as liquefied natural gas from the City's landfill, developing solar energy sources, and reaching out to developers and the community with more energy efficient building techniques.

Local Supporters: Mayor Golding and the City of San Diego, Brummitt Energy, Global Environmental Consulting, Poway Unified School District, Regional Water Quality Control Board, SAIC, San Diego Association of Governments, San Diego Earthworks, San Diego Regional Air Pollution Control District, San Diego Regional Energy Office, San Diego State University School of Business, San Diego Transit, University of California at San Diego Departments of Urban Studies and San Diego Dialogue, Sony Corporation, and ST-Microelectronics.

Federal Partners: Energy (lead agency), Commerce (Economic Development Administration), Environmental Protection Agency, Housing & Urban Development, and Transportation.

Tioga County, New York: Bringing Prosperity to Rural Communities

Description: This effort focuses on one rural county in South Central New York State that was overlooked by recent prosperity. To address these challenges, the county will develop an agri-tourism industry, revitalize waterfronts, spur new industry, and create schools that are centers of community life.

Local Supporters: County Government.

Federal Partners: Agriculture (lead agency), Commerce (Economic Development Administration), Education, Energy, Environmental Protection Agency, Health & Human Services, Housing & Urban Development, Transportation, Treasury, and U.S. Army Corps of Engineers.

Facilitating Interagency and Regional Partnerships

ISSUE: Many of the barriers to livability faced by communities are regional in nature: transportation, air and water quality, workforce development, and open space preservation. While local leaders increasingly recognize this, the organizational structure of the federal government makes it difficult to design and implement local strategies that cut across agency lines at a regional scale. The federal government can therefore take a number of actions to improve its ability to measure and recognize progress on a regional scale; train and reward federal employees to work in partnership with communities and other agencies; and improve interagency coordination of state and local planning requirements.

ACTION: The White House Task Force on Livable Communities will undertake three initiatives to develop a more effective and coordinated federal response to regional and local concerns about livability. The Task Force will work with federal agencies on the following:

- **Encouraging Agencies to Coordinate Performance Goals at a Regional Level.** The Government Performance and Results Act (GPRA) requires that every federal agency set goals, prepare strategic plans, and report to Congress on accomplishments. GPRA requires agencies to consider the ultimate impact of their work, not just their activities. The Office of Management and Budget (OMB) oversees agency implementation of GPRA. In instances where performance is best measured at a metropolitan or other regional level, OMB could use GPRA as a tool to encourage agencies to work together to express their goals and measure results at a regional level.

- **Giving Incentives and Training for Federal Workers to Engage in Collaboration.** Individual federal employees regularly collaborate with others. However, agencies could do more to reward interagency work and to train federal employees for this work. One strategy for increasing interagency collaboration and partnerships with communities and regions is for the Office of Personnel Management to work with individual agencies in designing new rating systems for federal employees and ensuring that agencies give full weight to this work in personnel evaluations. Interagency cooperation and collaborative work with state, regional, and local entities might be added to the core competencies in job descriptions for top federal officials. The importance of interagency and regional cooperation will be included in the Livable Communities Initiative's Community Livability Training efforts (see pages 47-50).

- **Aligning Federal Planning Requirements to Facilitate Integrated Regional Approaches**. In response to statutory requirements, federal agencies place various planning requirements on local and state governments. However, there is some degree of administrative flexibility to align planning processes more closely across agencies. It is also possible to make the plans, and the differences among them, more transparent and easily understood. For example, it may be possible to synchronize timing, align the geographic scale, cross-reference among plans, and create forums where the public could consider more than one plan at a time. These changes could allow local and state governments to address problems within a region more effectively.

A Partnership for Building Homes in America's Cities

ISSUE: While housing construction has proceeded at a healthy pace during this economic cycle, a recent study by the Joint Center for Housing Studies concluded that new home construction has largely bypassed central cities. In 1994, less than 10 percent of all single-family home construction occurred in cities. That same year, in many large cities, including Boston, Buffalo, Detroit, Hartford, Miami, Milwaukee, Providence, Rochester, New York, St. Louis, and Washington, D.C., less than 100 new homes were constructed. To build more livable communities, the benefits of home construction must come to the cities.

ACTION: In February 1999, Vice President Gore and Housing and Urban Development Secretary Cuomo announced a partnership with the U.S. Conference of Mayors and the National Association of Home Builders. They agreed to work together with cities, communities, builders, and bankers to build a million homes in cities over the next 10 years. In November 1999, HUD announced 14 pilot cities, with specific programs in each to identify and remove local regulatory and market barriers to produce 100,000 new housing units each year over the next 10 years. This public-private partnership will help breathe new life into cities as dynamic places to live, work, and play.

A Partnership to Analyze Federal Location Decisions

ISSUE: As the largest holder of real estate in the country, the federal government's decisions on where to locate its facilities can have either positive or negative impacts on the economic health of communities. More information, however, is needed to better understand how public buildings contribute to the economic health of the communities in which they are located and to explore the extent to which location and design affect how federal buildings can reinforce or undermine community vitality.

ACTION: The General Services Administration's (GSA) Center for Urban Development is partnering with the National Trust for Historic Preservation's National Main Street Center to develop a model to assess the economic impacts of federal location decisions in communities. The National Main Street Center is tapping into its network of 1,500 active Main Street programs to create a model that will gauge the effect of federal facilities on other downtown assets. With this model, GSA can provide data and analysis on its facilities to communities to enable local officials and federal agencies to make better design, planning, location, and development decisions – decisions that will help build a stronger sense of community.